How to Live a Meaningful Life

Also by Tim Sledge

Making Peace with Your Past (1992)

Moving Beyond Your Past (1994)

Goodbye Jesus: An Evangelical Preacher's Journey Beyond Faith (2018)

Four Disturbing Questions with One Simple Answer (2019)

You can contact Tim Sledge on his website, MovingTruths.com, where he shares insights for personal growth.

How to Live a Meaningful Life

Focusing on Things that Matter

Tim Sledge

How to Live a Meaningful Life: Focusing on Things that Matter

Copyright ©2019 by Tim Sledge. All Rights Reserved Worldwide

All rights reserved. No part of this book may be reproduced in any form or by any electronic or mechanical means including information storage and retrieval systems, without permission in writing from the author. The only exception is by a reviewer, who may quote short excerpts in a review.

Tim Sledge
www.MovingTruths.com

Printed in the United States of America

First Edition: August 2019

Insighting Growth Publications
Houston, Texas
www.IGrowPub.com

ISBN-13: 978-1-7333520-3-1 (Paperback)
ISBN-13: 978-1-7333520-4-8 (E-Book)
ISBN–13: 978-1-7333520-5-5 (Audiobook)

About the Author

Tim Sledge is a humanist writer and speaker whose mission is discovering and sharing insights for personal growth. You can read his latest articles and stay in touch via his website, MovingTruths.com.

Sledge is a former Southern Baptist pastor and author. After devoting his career as an evangelical preacher to leading and growing ministries in Illinois, Tennessee, New Jersey, and Arizona, he moved to a suburb of Houston, Texas, where, as senior pastor, he led his church to experience dramatic growth and wrote two books that launched a ground-breaking support group ministry. *Making Peace with Your Past* and *Moving Beyond Your Past* have now been in print for more than 25 years, and have been used as interactive guides for 20,000 support groups across the U.S.

At the peak of his ministerial career, a 10-year series of events led to a growing awareness that faith was no longer working for him. His journey into and out of faith is chronicled in *Goodbye Jesus: An Evangelical Preacher's Journey Beyond Faith*.

Table of Contents

Introduction 1
Truth 5
Introspection 15
Values 27
    Strength 33
    Kindness 47
    Truthfulness 53
    Humility 57
    Gratitude 63
    Generosity 67
    Love 75
Purpose 81
Expectancy 87
Pacing 91
Now 95

Relationships 103

Toxicity 113

Danger 123

Health 137

Serenity 139

Inspiration 143

Mantra 147

Epilogue 155

Endnotes 156

Introduction

In my spiritual autobiography, *Goodbye Jesus: An Evangelical Preacher's Journey Beyond Faith*, I shared my story of five decades of up-close involvement with churches, Christians, and ministers. I wrote of what it felt like to be a committed believer and a productive pastor. I did my best to journal my struggles and failures along with my accomplishments. But the heart of the story was my journey out of faith.

The breaking point occurred when I decided that no supernatural source was needed to explain the inconsistent results of belief that I had witnessed for decades in one church after another. It all made more sense when I understood that church—as impressive as it could be at times—is just one more human organization. The end of my faith was not far behind.

Walking away from Christianity entailed many losses, and what naturally followed was a process of grief. I lost not only my spiritual family, but long-in-place faith footings for meaning, purpose, and values were gone as well.

But there were some things I didn't lose. I was still drawn to searching for the deepest truths and the highest values in life. I was still interested in self-reflection. I continued to recognize the importance of perseverance and resilience. I still needed an explanation for the presence of evil in the world. Relationship skills were still important. Competence in dealing with failures, losses, and toxic emotions was still required. And I still wanted to engage in the lifelong quest to find and become my best self.

These issues continued to be important after leaving faith because they are vital concerns for any human life, and religion is not the only way to address them.

Without my prepackaged belief system and with these issues in mind, I faced a multitude of choices about what the new version of me would look like. I began to think for myself about how to build a meaningful life without God, faith, or religion, and this became a process of carefully considering what mattered to me in life.

I decided that if I could describe a religion-not-required way of finding meaning in life by focusing on things that really matter, it would be something worth sharing—especially if it could make sense and work for anyone, regardless of religious beliefs, political stance, personality type, lifestyle, or generational label.

This book is the result of the process described above. What I have written in these pages comes from my own thinking, experiences, and insights. No divine inspiration is claimed. But regardless of whether you're a free-thinking skeptic or a religious person, you can find something helpful here.

Introduction

There's no need for you to agree with me on everything. Some things that matter to me may not matter to you, and your things that matter list will likely include items not present in mine. That's good because I see this book as a launching pad for considering what matters most to you with the goal of finding your own ways to live a more intentional and more meaningful life.

And if you are currently at a point where some loss has prompted a reboot of your life, be encouraged by a story about starting over.

> A church in Europe was bombed during World War II. The most memorable part of the hollowed-out church building had been a stunningly beautiful, stained-glass window. In the days after the bombing, members of the church picked up the pieces of the shattered window and hid them away.

When the war was over, and the church was rebuilt, an artist was hired to create a new stained-glass design using the tiny broken fragments from the original window. When the artist's work was finished, everyone who saw the new window said it was more beautiful than the one it replaced.

After my life of faith collapsed, I picked up the broken pieces and tried to envision a new way of living. It took me years to think through what still mattered to me, but I like who I am today more than any previous version of me. I'm my own version of a stained-glass window rebuilt from broken pieces. If you too have been broken, I desire the same better-than-expected outcome for you.

I hope that in this book, you will discover new pathways toward meaning as you consider what matters most in your life.

When you are living out a meaningful purpose, you can flourish, and flourishing means a shortage of boredom, frequent surprise at how quickly time has passed, and a positive pull toward tomorrow.

Tim Sledge

Truth

Meaningful living requires focusing on what matters, and truth needs to be at the top of anyone's things that matter list because pursuing truth is what makes reality-based living possible.

We're living in a time when truth is often a moving target. Is that story on the news accurate or fake? Where did that social media post really come from? Is that online video a deep fake with frames doctored to make an innocent person look bad? You could argue that it's never been so difficult to know what's real and what isn't.

But knowing what is true has always been challenging—even before social media hacking, high tech video editing, and biased news reporting. Cognitive bias, fear of change, backward tribal thinking, and denial of the obvious are battle-hardened truth fighters.

Built-In Bias

One ever-present challenge to discerning what is true is wired into our brains. It's a built-in bias. We struggle to accept anything that conflicts with our existing beliefs. We are likely to place whatever disagrees with our preconceived opinions at the back of the line for thoughtful consideration. Or, we give such ideas no place in line at all.

This resistance to new ideas is likely an evolved survival technique. In a more primitive world where little was known about what makes things happen, it was easy to think that believing in the wrong god could get you struck by lightning. Eating a new kind of food or trying a new method of killing a wild beast for dinner might get you killed. With limited tools for analyzing new possibilities, it was safer to stick with what had been tried before. New ideas could be dangerous.

In many ways, things aren't that different today. Bad ideas on just about any subject shout for attention. If we naively believed and acted on every new idea we encountered, we would zigzag aimlessly about never accomplishing anything and looking stupid in the process. Hitching your wagon to something new and unknown could lead to a loss of money, job, or dignity.

There's still some value in trusting what you already think you know to be true, and it's a good thing not to be so open minded that your brains fall out. But if we're not careful, we can get stuck in time as we hold on to beliefs, concepts, and values taught to us in our formative years—not because they're true, but just because they represent the way things were first explained to us.

That's what happened with my religious faith. A belief system I learned as a child held a chunk of my thinking in a logic-resistant state for decades.

Reality is not a choice in a cafeteria line, but it's easy to live by a road rut mantra that says: I'll have the *everything is the way I've always understood it* casserole. And for dessert, I'll have the *eyes closed, don't want to look at the evidence* pie.

Fear-Driven Resistance

Our human hesitations can cloud reality as well. Some aspects of life may seem too frightening to accept as real. When paradigm-shifting change presses its way into our lives like a slow-moving glacier, our fear of what is different than what we've always known or want to be true can prompt us to metaphorically pull out a hairdryer, turn it to full heat, and point it at the encroaching mountain of ice. In other words, fear of change can lead to a fight with reality.

You cannot melt an iceberg with a hairdryer, but you can aim, blow hot air at it, then pretend it's melting. Wanting something to be true, needing something to be true, and fearing that the opposite might be what is correct—can all add up to what can become a chosen ignorance of what is accurate, real, and right.

Rapid, invasive change can incite fear, and such fear can push modern humans backward into primitive tribal thinking. There's strength in numbers, and fear-driven ignorance grows geometrically stronger when reinforced by a tribe of other people who think the same way.

We all have tribes, and that's not a bad thing. A tribe can provide a sense of safety and belonging. But if your tribe imposes boundaries on truth, and you refuse to listen to any voice outside your tribe, you will soon be imprisoned in a rigid thought cage with bars you cannot see. Tribal "truth" can be dangerously false, and its partner in crime is denial.

Disabling Denial

Denial is the friend of biased thinking, fear, backward tribal thinking, and willful ignorance. Practice denial long enough, and your views will harden like concrete—able to resist the toughest assaults by reality.

The antidote to dysfunctional denials of reality is a bold willingness to follow the truth wherever it leads. And on any truth-seeking journey, science is a great model for how to proceed.

That's right. I said science.

Science shows us how to override our penchant for resisting change to our way of thinking. It teaches us to ask, "What is the evidence that something is true?"

Science begins with a hypothesis, then looks for evidence pro and con. True science follows the evidence—even when it does not point to the desired outcome.

Science teaches us to get comfortable in living with tentative "conclusions" as we continue to take in new information. We cannot stop everything until we know everything, but we can work with the best information we have at any given time, and we can stay open to each new idea, experience, or insight. And if enough evidence is not available, science teaches us that it's okay to say: *I don't know*.

Science affirms the value of skepticism, and models not only a willingness to admit it when we don't have enough information to answer a particular question but also encourages a readiness to say, "I've changed my mind. The position I took a week ago (or a year ago or decades ago) is wrong."

Science teaches us to keep reassessing and learning, even when it means changing our minds.

Religion was humanity's first attempt to explain how things work as it filled in the blanks where understanding was lacking. The crops failed because the god of the harvest was angry. A disease outbreak was a punishment from a god. A frightening thunderstorm could be an ominous sign that it was time to sacrifice a virgin.

When science came along, offering better answers for why things happen, the answers were not always welcome. Religions tend to dislike competition in pronouncing what's true and what isn't.

In 1633, Galileo was condemned by the Roman Catholic Inquisition for promoting the theory of Nicolaus

Copernicus that the sun, not the earth, is the center of our solar system. The Church ordered Galileo not only to stop teaching the concept but also to stop believing it. More than 350 years later, after a 13-year investigation of Galileo's condemnation, the Vatican admitted he was right.

Be on the alert for a partnership with denial by any organization, ideology, or mindset that values tradition or "revealed" truth over evidential truth. A carefully crafted denial system can be seductive—one more reason to be skeptical, ask questions, and think critically.

I'm not advocating a Star Trek Vulcan style of thinking that is limited to cold logic. Our emotions matter and will often rightly affect what we do with truth. But we can profit by using the follow-the-evidence-anywhere attitude of science as our model for how we discover what is true.

Open-Minded Thinking

Reality is not a secret. You don't have to choose the right religion to discover what is real and true. You don't have to locate just the right guru who offers the only pathway to truth. You don't need to pay someone a sizable fee to learn the secret key to life. But you do have to open your mind.

Truth is accessible to anyone willing to examine the evidence and do the work necessary to comprehend. I'm not saying truth is always simple or that understanding things is always easy. Not everyone can master quantum physics. Some areas of knowledge are hard to grasp even if you're a specialist, and the worldwide body of human knowledge is now too large for any one of us to know everything. But I am saying that the basic truths about what's real and what isn't and what matters and what doesn't are not secrets available to only a select few.

Often, it's not that truths are beyond our grasp, it's that we're committed to the blinders we wear, and we don't want to take the time to stop and think about things we believe we already understand. Sometimes we're simply too lazy to ask questions and listen to the answers.

I'm opting for thinking that is open-minded and expectant—a mindset of readiness to learn something from even the most unlikely person, place, or thing. It's a posture that allows confidence in what I already know while still acknowledging I could be wrong about this or that. It's an attitude that looks forward to each discovery whether the source of the insight is ordinary or surprising.

Looking Deeper

Another lesson from science that is helpful in our search for truth is the value of looking deeper. Microscopes reveal tiny worlds we cannot see. Telescopes introduce us to the distant realms of space. Bacteria and black holes can't be seen just by gazing, but science finds ways to *see* the invisible.

Science helps us understand that what something initially appears to be is simply the most visible part of a more complex reality.

Consider a dining room table. When you look at it, you see a stationary, solid object. Although it looks solid, the table consists of millions of atoms with electrons whirling around at staggering speed. Between the electrons and the nucleus of each atom are microscopic—but proportionately huge—open spaces. Despite appearing solid, the dining room table is more empty space than anything else.

And that's not all. The table appears to be standing still, and, as an observable thing in the dining room, it is standing still. However, not only is it crammed full of zooming electrons, it's in a room on a planet that is spinning at 1,000 miles an hour while orbiting the sun at 67,000 miles an hour in a solar system circling the center of the Milky Way at over 400,000 miles an hour. The dining table appears to be a solid object that is standing still, and it is, but it isn't.

We can discover more of the truth about everything when we live with the awareness that all around us, there is more than initially meets the eye. And if something as simple as a wooden table is so much more than what it appears to be, then what about people?

Every person has a unique face, shape, and voice, but there's much more to every individual than what we immediately see and hear. Biology tells us we are made of trillions of tiny cells. Physics tells us that the cells in our bodies are made of atoms with protons, neutrons, and electrons inside. And when it comes to people, looking deeper is not just about MRIs and electron microscopes.

Each of us is unique not only in how we look and sound but also in who we are. It's a singularity shaped by inherited traits and by the life experiences that comprise an individual's personal story—information that may not be easily accessible. Knowing and understanding another person at a deeper level requires getting past protective walls by building trust, and it requires your willingness to be known. A relational toolbox loaded with empathy, curiosity, a willingness to listen, and patience is required. When you model the openness and safety you desire from others and use these relational tools with care, you will frequently observe the unvarnished identity of another person revealing itself in layers as trust develops through multiple interactions.

As we refine our skills for looking deeper and listening better and apply them to all aspects of life, our awareness of things that are true will expand. We will connect more significantly with the world and the people in it. And soon we will find ourselves living at a deeper level, more capable of taking in the richness of life.

Weighing the psychological implications of why we're prone to believe on not believe something, overcoming fear and denial, cultivating an open mindset, taking advantage of resources that enable us to see beneath the surface level, building relational skills like active listening, and thinking things through—all these apply as we make decisions about what is true or false, real or fake, and as we seek to know other people at a deeper level.

The alternative to a truth-seeking lifestyle is living without openness to learning, change, and growth—a way of life that can harden you into a brick made only of notions accepted long ago—viewpoints never reviewed or questioned. And when you are a metaphorical brick, the ever-learning and ever-changing world will pass you by.

Seeking all kinds of truth matters: facts about the physical world, understanding what's real and what isn't, deciding what really matters, discovering what makes other people who they are, and understanding yourself.

Life Principle

Seeking Truth Matters: Look deeper, be willing to change your mind, and follow the truth wherever it leads.

Introspection

It's hard to make progress in a quest for meaningful living if you don't have a good understanding of who you are. And if you think understanding yourself better than you do now is neither necessary nor possible, you assuredly have some work to do. When it comes to self-awareness, we all have work to do.

Knowing yourself requires more than a glance in the mirror. It's an ongoing introspective process, and it's hard work. Socrates is reported to have said, "The unexamined life is not worth living." And Robert Fulghum added, "The examined life is no picnic."[1]

To fully comprehend the ins and outs of who you are, you may need to experience the discomfort of examining traits you'd rather not acknowledge. You may feel worse before you feel better, but it's worth the effort and discomfort.

Knowing yourself is hard work, but it's also empowering, and it's a crucial element in the pursuit of a meaningful, reality-based life.

The first step toward understanding yourself better is taking note of some common barriers to self-awareness.

Discovering Blind Spots

The hardest thing to see is me. In fact, self-awareness is so challenging that it's possible to be unaware of behavioral traits that others spot within minutes of meeting you—this is called a blind spot.

When driving a car, it's hard to see the spot just behind you on the passenger side. It's called a blind spot because even with a neck-craning look and a glance at all your mirrors, you may miss a car lurking just behind you and to your side.

Some vehicles offer an electronic "blind spot checker" that lights up in the side-view mirror when there's a vehicle hiding in your blind spot. Too bad we don't have a personal blind spot alert app—one that can read your brain and output a warning to your smartphone.

However big or small, whatever your blind spots look like, knowing what they are and addressing them will help you grow. What you don't know *can* hurt you.

Not knowing who you are slows you down in life—like moving through a dimly lit room rather than one in which the lights are fully turned up.

Our blind spots are often hiding places for character flaws—areas that need work but are painful to face. And you could have a blind spot for some gift or talent you possess, a trait that's hidden from you, but obvious to others who know you well. Wouldn't that be nice to know and to use to your advantage?

Keep in mind that sometimes blind spots take cover behind our best traits. For example, you're intelligent, even gifted—that's positive—but your blind spot is that you tend to assume you're always right in a way that comes across as arrogance. Or, your kindness is what people love most about you—a positive trait—but your blind spot is that you are sometimes kind in a way that allows others to take advantage of you.

Finding your blind spots is not something you do alone. You need help—being hard for you to see is why they're called blind spots. You can look in your meditative mirror all you want and still miss a blind spot.

It's beneficial if you have a loving friend, relative, or partner who's shared innumerable experiences with you, has no ax to grind, is not jealous of you nor condescending, and is as courageous and honest as they are kind.

If no such personal acquaintance is available, consider a qualified professional counselor, and commit to enough sessions to make yourself known. You'll be surprised at the insights that become available to you within a few sessions if you are honest, open, and vulnerable. Don't let a lack of funds deter you. Be proactive. Some counselors will occasionally work with a client for a reduced rate as an act of service. Community counseling services may be available. If you cannot find a counselor, look for free support groups that can offer help.

Once you have identified a trusted individual who can help you see yourself better, you'll need to convince this blind spot revealer that you're ready to listen to whatever you need to hear and that you won't attack the messenger.

"Tell me something I don't know about myself" is a good place to start. Or, maybe you have a hunch about a blind spot of yours and want to be more specific in what you ask, for example: "Do you think I have a problem with x?"

It may take some coaxing to get your potential mirror person to tell you what they see, and how you respond to his or her first comments will likely determine the quality of further feedback. So, brace yourself and plan your response. "Thank you for your feedback," is a good reply.

If you think what is being said is not accurate, apply extra effort toward open-mindedness, keep listening, and ask clarifying questions. Is the person providing feedback someone who truly cares about you and has no hidden agenda? Does this person know you well? Is this someone who you generally regard as insightful? If the answer to all these questions is yes, seriously consider what this person is telling you.

If one item of feedback is all you're ready to hear, clearly communicate your desire to stop. "Thank you for your feedback. I need some time to process it."

Your internal response to the feedback could be an immediate recognition of its truth. You sort of knew it before you heard someone else say it and hearing it from a person who cares about you helped you acknowledge it. Or, the feedback could be a total surprise like the blaring horn you hear when you start pulling into the next lane with a car in your blind spot. If the information catches you off guard, don't panic—and don't immediately assume it's true or false.

If you doubt the accuracy of the feedback you've received, go to a second person who meets the same criteria as the first: has shared multiple and varied experiences with you, no ax to grind, not jealous, not condescending, kind, honest, and courageous.

Here's a good intro for your second blind spot feedback conversation. "I'm on a reflective journey—trying to understand myself better—and I'm working to learn more about myself and make some improvements. I've gotten feedback from one person, and I'd like to bounce it off you." Be sure you don't say, "You don't think I have a problem with (whatever the first person said about you), do you?"

What's important is to choose someone who is not only kind but also sees more value in telling you the truth than in making you feel good in the moment. If you've picked the wrong person, he or she may tell you what you want to hear—even while knowing the feedback you received from your first conversation was true.

Your spouse or life partner may have been alerting you to

one or more blind spots for a while, and a new openness to his or her input could be a good starting place. Your partner may be your best source of feedback if you can be open and vulnerable enough to listen and can do so without retaliating.

Whoever your feedback person is, be sensitive to their need for personal boundaries. Communicate that you want him or her to be comfortable with the conversation. Be sensitive to the possibility that she or he may be ready to give you feedback in certain areas, but not in others.

Only you can decide if the feedback you receive about yourself is accurate. Be cautious about discrediting similar messages from multiple people who know you well and care for you deeply—they are likely to contain some truth.

If you're tempted to declare yourself blind spot free, be especially careful, because one of the ways we keep our blind spots operational is denial.

Dealing with Denial

Simon Cowell was notorious for excoriating contestants who showed up to try out for the American Idol television show even though they were awful singers. It happened so often that you could anticipate the disbelief, the shattered look, and the process of turning on the judges by the contestant who could not sing a note. Clearly, prior to the audition—and possibly even afterward—the aspiring vocal star on the receiving end of Cowell's derision really believed he or she could sing like an angel—a perfect example of denial.

These professional singer wannabes were likely failed by friends and loved ones who thought it better to help them feel they were good at something rather than telling them the truth: "You can't sing, and doing it for fun is fine, but you need to try something else for a career."

When you receive false information about who you are and what you're good at—especially from one or more key people in your life—if it goes on long enough, it may be very hard to stop believing what you've been told. This can be the case even when it's obvious to just about everyone else that what you believe about yourself isn't true.

Denial is the head cheerleader for our blind spots. Denial stares truth down daily. Denial protects us from hearing what we do not want to hear and seeing what we do not want to see.

Why would anyone want to live in denial? Here's one motivation: fear of the feelings that will follow if you face the truth.

Facing Feelings

Our need to maintain blind spots and stay in denial may be connected to an unwillingness to experience each of the emotions that come our way. It's natural to resist pain, but fear of experiencing emotional pain can become a detrimental driving force. Turning your back on your emotions empowers and energizes them for a long-running attack on you.

This truth smacked me in the face in 1988, when I spent five days at The Meadows, a recovery facility in Wickenburg, Arizona. I went there to gather material for a sermon series at the church I pastored but ended up doing work as an adult child of an alcoholic.

It was a life-altering week of small group therapy, and the question I heard over and over was, "How does that make you feel?"

At first, I'd answer with something like, "I think the situation I'm in is a difficult one." The group leader would respond, "You didn't answer the question. How does that make you feel?"

My answers were sourced from thinking more than feeling. My group leader was working to help me zero in on one or more basic emotions—shame, guilt, anger, sadness, fear, pain, loneliness, peace, or joy.

After a few days in the group, I started to get the hang of it, but it wasn't easy. I learned better, more accurate answers like, "I'm feeling sad right now," or "I feel angry about that," or "I'm feeling joy."

In those few days, I discovered I had spent a lifetime shelving away many of the emotions inside me. That week, I learned to say no to the fear of owning what I was feeling and to embrace even my negative emotions. I learned that when I embraced a downbeat emotion, when I gave it a voice, I reduced its power, and could more easily let it go.

And I learned that a key aspect of emotional health is being able to identify what you are feeling at a given moment.

If you're feeling angry, it's good to be in touch with the anger and to think about why you are angry. If you're feeling shame, it's good to be able to concede that is what you're feeling and to reflect on where the shame is coming from. If you're feeling joy, but cannot acknowledge it, that's an issue to overcome, and the starting point in overcoming is asking "Why?"

Becoming willing to feel your emotions—whatever they are—empowers you to break out of the prison of denial, to see your blind spots, to accept what needs to be accepted, and to work on changing what needs to be changed. Embracing your pain allows you to let it go.

If you have a major backlog of unreleased emotional pain, you may need help in your first steps toward letting it go. This is especially true if you are a victim of violence or some other form of abusive behavior. Post-Traumatic Stress Syndrome is real and dealing with it is not a do-it-yourself project. The more intense the pain and the longer you've kept it bottled, the greater the likelihood that help is needed. Find a qualified therapist if you need assistance.

Looking Deeper

Discovering blind spots and facing our feelings are just

two ways we can know ourselves better.

Another helpful tool for increasing self-awareness is the Myers-Briggs Indicator personality inventory which can be taken online with results delivered in a four-letter description of one of 16 personality types. A key idea behind the Myers-Briggs Indicator test is that much of human behavior that appears to be random is actually the result of differences in how individuals use perception to become aware of people, things, events, and ideas as well as differences in how they make judgments about what they perceive. The way an individual perceives and judges can point to likely interests, reactions, values, and skills. Your four-letter Myers-Briggs Indicator personality type can help you evaluate potential fulfillment in a variety of situations, including relationships and vocational work. There are no bad personality types—the test is designed to help you understand yourself better.[2]

To take the Myers-Briggs Indicator inventory online, Google "Myers Briggs Test." You'll find a number of sites where you can take the inventory and learn your personality type right after answering the last question

Reading about issues we face, participating in support or therapy groups, and one-to-one counseling are other ways we can understand ourselves better. Regardless of the methods utilized, one task will always be required—looking deeper.

Looking deeper within is the only way we will ever see our

true selves—and since we are constantly evolving and reacting to new experiences, as we look inward, we are not looking at a stationary target. This means that we need to get comfortable with an introspective lifestyle and learn to regard it not like a painful root canal—something you just want to be over with—but rather, as a good way to live.

Seeing introspection as a normal part of a meaningful life doesn't mean you should head for a monastery and spend every waking hour navel-gazing. If introspection is all you do, you're doing it too much.

Engaging in introspection does not mean you are selfish, self-absorbed, or narcissistic. On the contrary; one of the intended results of knowing yourself better is how this awareness can positively affect your interactions with other people—including an increase in your ability to respond to others with sensitivity.

Personal growth occurs as you learn more about your uniqueness, history, strengths, weaknesses, unresolved issues, and even your dark side—the other "you" that appears under stress. This growth takes place as you disable your blind spots, say no to denial, and move beyond the fear of experiencing your emotions. Growth occurs as you become more willing to see yourself as you really are.

Curiosity turned inward leads to self-awareness, and self-awareness is one of the things that really matter, one of the building blocks of a meaningful life.

Life Principle

Self-Awareness Matters: Never stop learning about who you are—even when doing so is challenging or painful.

Values

Do values matter if no God is watching and there is no life beyond this one? Christians commonly answer this question with a no. They say that if God does not exist and life ends at death, there's no reason not to do whatever you please.

But laws, societal norms, and common reactions to certain behaviors still exist when you don't believe in God or an afterlife. And doing whatever you feel like doing—depending on what it is you feel like doing—could be barbaric, uncivilized, and illegal.

Theoretically, one could contend that the best strategy—when you believe neither in God nor life after death—is to act like you are expected to act when others are watching. Then, when no one is looking, do whatever you choose, whatever feels good to you and advances your own interests—even if it includes things like cheating, stealing, or lying.

You could live this way, and some people do, but we have an ample supply of adjectives for them—double-dealing, deceptive, hypocritical, and insincere. Such people are inconsistent. We can't depend on them. They don't do what they say they'll do. They master a public persona that hides their true identity.

These individuals may push their way into positions of power, and can even win a misplaced respect from others, but, duplicitous, what-you-see-is-not-what-you-get people are not the kind of people you want your children to be. At least, I hope that's how you feel, because if it's not, you too may be broken.

Something goes wrong in us when we nurture a hidden identity that is drastically different from how we portray ourselves to other people.

I understand that any of us can find ourselves in a situation where some nuanced adjustment in our persona is temporarily made to deal with conditions that limit our options for responding. I recognize that hard-to-shake societal expectations related to gender, ethnicity, and sexuality can sometimes make it hard to fully express one's true identity. But these instances are not what I'm referring to.

I'm alluding to a person who consistently and willfully decides to act out a false identity to control and manipulate other people. If you become such a person—even if your duplicity is not discovered—living your life is at least one component of your just punishment. If you're not a sociopath, then you have a conscience, and living with the constant cognitive dissonance that you create by being two different people is stressful and wearisome.

But my argument that values matter when faith in God is gone is not just that breaking the basic rules of life isn't smart, socially acceptable, or safe. It's not just that consistently and intentionally portraying a personal integrity that doesn't exist is dishonorable and exhausting.

The more important point is that when one stops believing in God and an afterlife, all inner impulses to be and do good and the desire to respect the lives and property of other people, do not automatically disappear into thin air.

When I stopped believing in any religion or God, I didn't stop wanting to be a good person. I just had to figure out what being a good person looked like for me in my new approach to life.

I did stop believing it's necessary to pray multiple times each day—I stopped praying at all. I did cease observing Sundays as a day to attend worship services. I did stop looking to the Bible as the source for my core values. I did go through a period of evaluating what I believed about right and wrong—a relatively short, adolescent-like, trial-and-error phase that helped me decide where to set my new boundaries.

When the dust settled, my new list of core values did not look that different from my old one. I had not stopped wanting to become the best possible version of myself. I had not given up on a quest for value-driven living. And in many ways, I felt more genuinely myself—more authentic—than at any previous time in my life.

Not believing in God does not wipe out a desire to build character, a willingness to learn from mistakes, and a search for what is highest and best. And, the absence of faith does not automatically cause the moral quality of one's life to decline.

When religious people tell me it's not possible for anyone to live by meaningful core values without believing in God, it makes me think of a kid on a bike with training wheels. He sees his friend riding on two wheels for the first time and shouts, "You can't ride like that!"

Actually, you can ride like that, and it's a liberating way to move ahead.

Every single day, all kinds of people who have no commitment to some other group's "one true religion" make choices to excel in their thoughts, actions, and relationships—and "all kinds of people" includes humanists, skeptics, agnostics, and atheists.

In my view, our desire to be good and do good comes not from God, but from our evolved awareness that we need to cooperate with other people, from our childhood training, and from our life experiences.

But regardless of your opinion on where a desire to be good comes from, you can find value in what I have to say about values in the following pages. In the next seven chapters, you'll find a discussion of values that matter—seven core values, which in my view, make sense for everyone and are essential for meaningful living.

In developing my list of core values, I thought about what I learned from my former Christian faith—the personal values that still make sense. I thought about principles that I saw at work in support groups I led or participated in over the years, principles that helped people who were emotionally wounded or were struggling in some other way. I thought about my own challenges to becoming a better person, and what has helped and hindered me. I also thought about how balance is important, and I've attempted to keep things simple.

I am writing from my new point of view as a non-believer, but I think anyone can find something helpful in what I have to share about being strong, kind, truthful, humble, grateful, generous, and loving.

Life Principle

Values Matter: Build personal character on core values that work for everyone.

Strength

When I was a committed Christian, I looked to God for strength. I studied the Bible and did my best to obey its commandments. I prayed. I worshipped. I attempted to practice a sense of the presence of God. And through all these activities, I believed that I received a strength that comes *only* from God.

I see things differently now. Since I no longer believe that a personal, interactive God exists, I view any strength that follows the practice of acts of religious faith as coming from within the individual and from the encouragement of other practitioners of the faith—not from a benevolent deity. So, part of my new, secular, meaningful-life mindset is the belief that we must each find our own inner strength.

But if you are a person of faith, please don't assume that what I have to say about strength doesn't apply to you. I still recognize the need for help outside myself. I don't look to any deity for aid, but I'm not afraid to seek help from family and friends, and I find strength in their support. Isn't that something that anyone—regardless of faith or lack of it—should do?

And no matter how many outside sources of strength we

believe in and appeal to, I think that each of us needs to recognize, build, and maintain our own inner core of strength.

Here's a good place to start. Think of a time in your life when you did something extremely difficult. Maybe it was standing up to an intimidating person. Perhaps it was working through a terrible loss in your life. Maybe it was walking away from a toxic relationship. Or, you climbed out of a financial hole and started over. Possibly, it was a marathon run, an educational achievement, or some other demanding goal you set and accomplished.

As you think about how you successfully managed this difficult challenge, loss, or trauma in the past, consider this question: What was the source of your strength?

Can you acknowledge that *you* were strong in the situation?

Can you concede that it was *your* strength that kept you going—even if others were helping you along the way? Decisions were made that only *you* could make. Actions were taken that only *you* could take. *You* took each step. *You* were strong.

Is it hard to acknowledge that *you* were strong at a crucial juncture in your life?

I spent decades listening to religious teachings telling me, over and over, that I was inherently weak and could only be strong with God's help. Credit for any achievement—large or small—was to be given to God alone, and I was constantly on the alert to not give too much standing to my own strength and resolve. So, if you find it hard to acknowledge your strength, I understand.

Life at home can inflict similar damage. If you grew up with a parent who constantly criticized, the negative words you heard countless times may still haunt you and make it hard to see yourself as strong. Growing up with constant criticism makes it difficult to believe in your own value, insights, and strength.

When religious warnings or parental put-downs are echoing in your thoughts, acknowledging your own strength will be challenging—but challenging does not mean impossible.

I'm learning to visualize a core of strength within myself. I know that who I am is in my brain, and I know my brain is in my head, but—as unscientific as it may be—I find it more helpful when I imagine that my core of strength is in my gut. It's not logical. It just works for me.

When I feel disheartened, afraid, or overwhelmed, I visualize my inner core of strength. I remind myself of times in the past when I acted with strength, and I remind myself that I am tough.

I'm not Superman, but I am strong, and I'm guessing you are too—at least, you can be with the right mindset.

Strength Components

A bulging bicep is an obvious indicator of a type of physical strength. A triathlon medal testifies to the strength of physical endurance. But what are the signs of inner strength? What does inner strength look like? I'm proposing that inner strength has at least four key components: integrity, self-reliance, determination, and resilience.

Integrity

Integrity is about choosing to do the right thing—regardless of the cost. It's also about being genuine and authentic in how you present yourself—a basic consistency in who you think you are, who you say you are, and what you do.

If integrity were easy, everyone would possess it, but it's not easy—there are so many things working against it.

Surrendering your integrity can be especially tempting when you're in a competitive environment with rule-breaking pressure from higher-ups. And even without pressure from superiors, you may fear being left behind. And this fear can tempt you to create another version of yourself—to embellish your story, your credentials, and your character.

When you do take a stand for what's right, and you're in the minority, there will likely be pressure to "let this one slide." But the one you let slide probably won't be the last one. You can expect future challenges to compromise, and if you keep "letting them slide," your integrity will slip away.

It's easy to go with the flow, but if the flow takes a wrong turn—well, it's the flow, and you're in it. The exits are hard to find.

Living with integrity is a challenge, but not unattainable. I'm not talking about perfection. It's normal to have some differences in your private and public personas. And it's normal to look different than your best self when you're under tremendous stress.

It's also normal to make some mistakes. People with integrity sometimes make bad choices that violate their core values, and such lapses are characterized by varying levels of intentionality. When bad behavior seduces us, we're rarely completely unaware of what's occurring, but when it's all over, we may still find ourselves sincerely asking, "How on earth did that happen?"

While not always true in the realm of public opinion, in the meaning-driven-life view of things, you don't get just one chance at integrity. Authenticity can restart and resume when you acknowledge inappropriate behavior, take responsibility, make amends, and get back in sync with your core values. You don't get just one chance, but it will be hard for others to believe in you if you're constantly violating your values and asking for a chance to start over.

Having integrity doesn't mean you never change

directions. As we experience life, learn, and grow, we gain new information that may lead to changes in values, goals, and purpose. Evolving in your identity is a good change and not the same thing as living with carefully constructed, multiple versions of yourself.

Remember that integrity is a kind of wholeness. When lines of code in a software application are missing or corrupted, and the application stops working properly, the software is said to have lost its integrity.

Self-Reliance

Self-reliance is another component of inner strength. Being self-reliant doesn't mean you can't follow a leader, keep your opinion to yourself when appropriate, or let someone else take center stage. Self-reliance doesn't mean you can only work alone or that you never need help from anyone else. Being self-reliant doesn't mean you think you're always right and believe everyone else is wrong.

Being self-reliant does mean you have developed an inner voice that says, "I can depend on me," and you refuse to let other people, institutions, or events define you or take control of your life.

Learning to stand on your own two feet doesn't mean you can't lean on someone else when you need to. It does mean that someone can lean on you without knocking you down.

You can be self-reliant as an introvert or an extrovert, female or male, old or young. It's not about age, gender, or personality type. It's about knowing who you are, being grounded by your integrity, and taking responsibility for the direction of your own life.

At the same time, developing self-reliance and having it recognized by others may be more challenging based on your gender, age, or personality type. For example, self-reliance may be valued more if you're male than female. And if you've been expected to be dependent all your life—regardless of the reason—developing self-reliance will likely be a challenging task that requires extra effort, but if you are determined enough, you can still do it.

Determination

Determination is the third component of inner strength. Determined people persist and stay on course, even when a hundred things get in the way. Determined people see obstacles as problems to be solved. And if they do get sidetracked, their determination soon has them back on course.

Determination is what you need when giving up looks inviting. As is true with integrity, being determined—to get where you want to go, to reach your goals, and to see your dreams come true—does not mean you never change. A mid-course correction is not the same as giving up.

Determined people do things that have never been done before—like sending astronauts to the moon or developing a new drug for stroke victims. Determination sends a firefighter into a burning building to save someone when it looks like an impossible task. Determination takes an Olympic athlete to world-class levels of performance.

Determined people do "small" things too, things you don't read about in the newspaper, but feats that are good news to the individuals they affect. Determined people are not always loud and standing at the front of the room. Theirs may be a quiet determination that escapes attention but still gets the job done.

Determined people have a positive impact on the lives of people they teach, coach, counsel, parent, inspire, lead, and befriend.

A determined attitude is well set on a foundation of integrity and self-reliance. But when determination meets its match, when things fall apart, and starting over is the only option, one other component of strength is needed.

Resilience

Simply stated, resilience means getting up when you fall down. Toddlers model resilience. They fall and get back up over and over. Sometimes they cry and need to be picked up to be comforted. But then they try again. Toddlers accept falling as part of their normal routine. That's how they learn to walk.

In adult life, resilience means you always find a way to start over after experiencing a setback or loss—no matter how discouraging, debilitating, or tragic it was. Resilience means you can adapt when the floor falls out from under you. If you must, you find a way to learn new skills, to start a new career, to make a better attempt at marriage—whatever it takes to start over and rebuild.

When life backs you into a corner and has almost convinced you there's no way out, resilience allows you to change your thinking, your attitude, and your behavior—and get going again.

Resilience means you can live in the present because you refuse to get stuck in the pain, the irony, or the indignity of past losses and mistakes.

Strength and Courage

Courage is the willingness to do something you know you need to do regardless of how frightening it is, and that requires strength.

Strength and courage feed one another. You need strength to be courageous, but each time you act with courage, you get a little stronger.

When you add courage to the strength of integrity, self-reliance, determination, and resilience, you can see dramatic results. You can stand up for what is right, even under pressure. You can do things you never thought possible. You can persist when others give up. And you can bounce back when everyone thought you were done.

Strength Training

How do you build inner strength? Here are three simple

suggestions.

Do What You Want to Become

Life teaches us that the way to get better at something is by doing it—over and over—and learning from our trial-and-error experiences.

Practicing integrity builds integrity. Choosing an attitude of self-reliance—in one situation after another—builds self-reliance. Persisting in persistence builds your determination muscle. Getting up—one more time—when you have fallen down in life builds resiliency.

You get stronger by being strong—one situation at a time.

Challenge Yourself

You can increase your physical strength—over time—by regularly lifting progressively heavier weights. Inner strength is no different because it too increases as you push yourself beyond what is easy.

Here's a good place to start. Do something you are afraid to do. I'm not recommending bungee jumping or sky diving. Keep safety in mind, but choose to do something that could fail, something that challenges you, something you want to do but are afraid of doing.

Maybe you decide to take a class in public speaking. Maybe it's taking a trip on your own. Maybe you finally sign up on that dating service. Maybe it's deciding you're willing to chair a committee on which you serve. It can be something than anyone else would consider a trivial matter, but to you, it's not—it's a challenge because it's something you fear.

You may or may not succeed in your first attempt, but either way, you will be moving away from fear. And you can always learn from your mistakes and try again until you get it right.

If you succeed—wonderful! If not, don't think of your activity as a failure. Instead, let your response to the outcome be your measure of success. Pat yourself on the back for giving it a go, then challenge yourself again.

Never Stop Learning

Learning increases knowledge, and knowledge makes you stronger.

In your quest for knowledge, self-awareness is foundational. Become an avid student of your own distinctiveness. Learning about yourself, your gifts, your blind spots, and the areas where you need to grow are all important. Make a habit of reviewing the self-awareness chapter in this book.

With self-awareness as your springboard, cultivate an inquisitiveness about all kinds of things. Increase your awareness of all that surrounds you: the universe, the earth, your culture, your work, your friends, and your family. Learn all you can about what makes other people who they are.

Observe. Listen intently. Ask questions.

This isn't about comparing your learning power to someone else's. It's about getting out of auto-pilot mode, looking at life with more curiosity, and paying more attention to what you see.

Knowledge decreases helplessness, and when you're moving away from helplessness, you're getting stronger.

Strength Awareness

If you have an audio loop in your brain that keeps telling you how weak you are, you need to replace it immediately! I would like you to begin thinking of yourself as a strong person right now. Here's how to get started. It's something I mentioned a few pages earlier—thinking back to times in your life when you were strong.

Think again about occasions when you did something that was extremely difficult—things like standing up to an intimidating person, working through a terrible loss, walking away from a toxic relationship, climbing out of a financial hole, or completing a challenging task like an educational achievement, a marathon run, or some other hard-to-achieve goal you set for yourself.

As you think about these times in the past when you acted with inner strength, pick the event that moves you the most when you remember it. Create a mental picture of yourself at that moment in time when you were strong.

Think of this mental image often and use the memory of the strength you displayed in this past event to help you consistently see yourself as a person with a core of inner strength, a person who is growing stronger day by day.

Core Value

Strength: Visualize your inner core of strength and practice strength training to build integrity, self-reliance, determination, and resilience.

Kindness

Kind is not a word you would normally look up in a dictionary, but if you did, you would find multiple synonyms—words like affectionate, benevolent, caring, considerate, friendly, generous, gentle, helpful, sympathetic, and warm.

I'm up for being on the receiving end of all these traits as often as possible. Aren't you? I want my life to intersect with kind people. It's a no brainer.

I consider myself a kind person and would like to think I'm always as ready to give kindness as I am to receive it. But sometimes, my selfish side gets in the way. Sometimes I'm tired. Sometimes I'm not paying attention. And some people are harder to be nice to than others. So, I need to keep working at being a kind person.

Even if kindness seems to be part of your DNA, you can profit from improving your kindness quotient—the ability to be kind to all types of people in all kinds of situations.

Components of Kindness
It's helpful to know what we're aiming for as we seek to display more kindness. I'm focusing on four components of kindness.

Respect

Treating another person with respect is a form of kindness. Respecting someone doesn't mean you agree with them. You don't even have to like someone to show them respect.

A measure of humility is helpful as we attempt to show respect for other people: their existence, their space, their boundaries, their rights, their property, their time, their privacy, their struggles, their experience, their views, and where they are in their journey.

After my convictions first changed from faith to non-belief, I went through a period of intolerance for people who still believed the things I had believed for most of my life. Gradually, I recognized the need to be more accepting. Today, when I meet a person of faith who can neither understand nor respect my current lack of belief in any religion or God, I try to see the former version of me in that individual—something that helps me to be more tolerant and to communicate more respect.

Even when someone is vastly different from any past or present version of me, even when I have no way of relating to how they view life, I can still choose to treat them with respect.

There are limits. I do not require myself to respect the behavior of abusive people. I will not respect hateful ignorance, racism, or other kinds of intolerance. I can choose—with full confidence in the quality of my character—to avoid or confront such people and attitudes. In these situations, strength and courage may be more important than kindness. But I want to be cautious and reluctant about deciding that avoidance or confrontation are the only options available.

Empathy

Before I label someone as beyond hope of change, beyond growth, beyond responsiveness to acts of kindness, and worthy of avoidance or confrontation, I want to put myself in their shoes.

Trying to see how things look through the eyes of someone I'm interacting with—empathy—is a component of kindness.

The starting point for understanding how life looks to another person is listening—without judgment.

If I can attain a measure of success in seeing things through another person's eyes, I may understand that individual's position better, and I may find more inner strength to show the kindness of respect.

It's more than understanding another person's views on politics, religion, or life in general. Empathy is about trying to understand how another person feels given the situation they are in. It's about thinking of what I would need or want if I were in the same state, but's it's more than that. It's about trying to learn whether this person needs are the same, similar, or different than what I would need in the same circumstances.

And sometimes, empathy means a willingness to help even when the help is not merited, to show respect when it may not be deserved, to be supportive when it would probably be okay to say, "You're on your own."

Patience
Patience is an expression of kindness and a by-product of empathy. As I understand someone better, I may find it easier to be patient with their behavior.

If patience were a traffic sign, it would read "Slow."

Patience is about decelerating to a slower pace because someone else needs me to. Saying yes to patience is saying no to a driven pattern of thinking, a racing mind, and the constant feeling that I'm running late. Slowing down allows us to listen better, to get onto the same page, to connect.

Children need our patience. Spouses and partners need our patience. Aging parents need it. People who are hurting need patience. And we need to learn to be patient with ourselves.

Forgiveness
When we have been hurt or betrayed, when it's hard to see anything good about how someone has treated us, respect, patience, and empathy may not be enough. Forgiveness may be the only way of moving forward.

Forgiving another person is an act of kindness—toward the other person, but also toward yourself. You do yourself a favor when you let go of the weight of resentment and the negative feelings that accompany it.

I can think of things I've done that probably did not deserve forgiveness, but the offended person chose to forgive me anyway, and I'm deeply grateful. I want to be the kind of person who forgives even when I could convince myself that the other person doesn't deserve it.

Forgiveness does not mean minimizing the wrongness of the act you are forgiving. I can forgive someone and keep my boundaries on alert if I see indications the offense may be repeated. I may even choose to distance myself for protection, but I can still forgive.

In the course of our reasonably healthy relationships, forgiveness will be a two-way street, a way of coping with our human imperfections, our bursts of self-centeredness, and our occasional fearful need to take charge of things that are not ours to control.

Forgetting how someone wronged you may not be possible since it's hard to control what we forget. But forgiveness is possible, and it's an action that can enable a relationship to continue when it would have otherwise ended.

Kindness with Strength

Kindness works best in partnership with a confident inner strength. Something's missing if you're kind only because you're afraid to be any other way.

Courageous kindness sets and maintains personal boundaries. It says no to being victimized or taken advantage of by others. If you're interacting with someone who regards kindness as weakness, your strength and your boundaries are what they need to see.

And sometimes you need to stand your ground not because the other person is an abuser or a bully, but just because it's important for the other person to know where you stand. Sometimes the kindest thing you can do for another person, and for yourself, is to be strong enough and courageous enough to speak the truth, even though it's painful for you and for the person you are speaking to.

At other times, the strongest, most courageous thing you can do is to kindly choose silence when everything in you wants to shout your frustration, fear, or pain.

Core Value

Kindness: Keep building your kindness quotient as you practice respect, empathy, patience, and forgiveness while remembering that kindness works best in partnership with a confident inner strength.

Truthfulness

We humans have learned to survive by cooperating, sharing resources, and working together—all activities that require effective communication.

Truthfulness is what makes communication work. Lying—the distortion, replacement, or strategic omission of accurate information—damages the value of language and can lead to a failure to communicate.

When communication breaks down, whatever human endeavor it is supporting deteriorates, whether it is a business deal, peace negotiations, or a close relationship.

My meaningful living mindset is concerned not only with finding out what is true, but also with telling the truth. And it sees truthfulness as one of the basic building blocks for positive and productive human interactions.

Truthfulness is the foundation for meaningful trust in all relationships. It's the basis for the emotional intimacy that occurs when you develop a close relationship that has significance, depth, and resilience.

As imperfect humans, we all fudge on the truth

occasionally. The niceties of social interaction can create grey area conflicts between politeness and truthfulness. A quick response in a stressful moment—upon later reflection—may reveal itself to have been less than truthful.

Adopting truthfulness as a core value does not mean you are aiming for perfection, but it does mean you are aspiring to make truthfulness habitual.

Truthfulness is a foundational character trait, a reference point for the kind of person you are, and a way that others decide whether they can count on you.

If you're known for not telling the truth, you have a serious handicap—you cannot be trusted. And if you can't be trusted, this gap in your character will affect your work, your friendships, and your deepest, most important connections with other people.

From a logical standpoint, truthfulness makes sense. So, why is lying so frequently a tempting choice?

A lie is a shortcut—an easy way to get through an awkward moment and a convenient avoidance technique.

We lie to avoid embarrassment. We lie to avoid facing consequences of previous actions. We lie to avoid what we don't want to do. And some people lie to manipulate.

But telling a lie is like taking out a loan you can't pay back.

Truthfulness

Lying erodes trust. It damages, and sometimes, ends relationships.

It's telling that even liars don't like to be lied to—the reasons: accurate information is crucial to whatever you are undertaking in life and being lied to feels devaluing.

Lies are used to dodge, hide, and confuse. Being on the receiving end of a lie points you right when you should go left. A lie creates anxiety when there is nothing to worry about. A lie convinces you to let your guard down just when you should be alert.

Not every lie is an act of evil, but according to author and psychiatrist Scott Peck, where evil is present, you will always find lying.[3]

Truthfulness is tied to the strength of integrity. Truthfulness requires courage. This is about where we aim, and when it comes to telling the truth, we need to aim high.

How we tell the truth is also important. Truthfulness is no excuse for a lack of kindness. Tone, timing, and discretion apply to how we tell the truth. And with those we love, truth should never be weaponized but should be delivered with sensitivity and care.

Core Value

Truthfulness: Tell the truth with strength, courage, and kindness.

Humility

Humility is an elusive target. No matter how hard you work to attain humility, you can never claim you've achieved it. "I've mastered humility," doesn't sound like something a humble person would say. It sounds like something an arrogant person would say, and arrogance is the opposite of humility.

Humility is a virtue best attributed to you by someone else—and not your public relations person. If you think you're humble, you should keep it to yourself.

But how do you work at being humble?

One of my friends, in a sincere effort to be humble, would never accept a compliment. Rather, he would downplay or deny the significance of any accolade sent his way. The result: The one giving the praise would repeat it with even greater enthusiasm—sometimes more than once—trying to make sure the compliment was properly delivered and received.

My friend's sincere effort at humility backfired and drew more attention to himself. Trying to be humble can be like trying to forget something—the more you think about it, the more you remember it.

How can we attain a virtue so elusive as humility?

And how much humility is enough? If striving for humility is not your own idea—if it's an externally imposed command or preachment—it's easy to feel guilty for not being humble enough just when you are at a point of healthy self-esteem. A guilt-driven effort at humility can become a whack-a-mole hammer poised to smack down any sense of healthy pride about a meaningful accomplishment.

Surely the road to humility is not for the faint-hearted!

I'm a long way from any semblance of mastering humility, but I do know one way to work toward it: Place your focus not on attaining humility, but on gaining and keeping a healthy perspective about your place in the big scheme of things.

You can start by going outside on a clear night and pondering the stars. Think about the massive size of the universe, our short tenure on this earth, and the limited impact any of us will have on the grand scheme of things.

Some will be fortunate enough to have some positive impact on a few contemporaries. Some of us will manage to make contributions that outlive us. If we are parents, our children are likely to be our best contributions to the future.

Despite all our efforts, each of us is so minuscule and

Humility

insignificant. This awareness can be discouraging, even overwhelming. It could lead you to decide that nothing you do has any significance and that all your efforts—along with life itself—are meaningless.

I must admit that it felt good to believe my actions would have consequences in another life beyond this one. It felt good to think of life on earth as the blink of an eye compared to eternity in heaven. Those assumptions felt good, but the faith that empowered them is no longer believable for me.

Recognizing the limited scope and significance of my finite life on earth makes humility a little easier than when I believed the God of the universe had personally called me to be a minister and was preparing an eternal home in heaven for me.

With or without religious faith, each of us is only a tiny speck in the world, and there's so much we don't know. Some subjects are complete mysteries and are likely to remain that way as long as you and I live.

If you still practice the faith I once followed, the promise of a God who knows you better than you know yourself and is preparing a place for you in heaven may help ward off feelings of insignificance. But if you're aiming for humility, it might be helpful to remember that—by the most conservative estimate—there will be hundreds of millions of individuals in heaven. Your faith tells you that Jesus loves you, died for you, and is listening to your prayers. But the same is true for incalculable millions, and until your anticipated Q&A session with God in heaven, you're just as in the dark as the rest of us about so many things. Recognizing these facts might help you keep things in perspective.

As a non-believer, I choose not to be overwhelmed by a zoomed-out view of how insignificant my life is, and by the scope of the things I'll never know. Instead, I choose to let this awareness be a source of humility. In my view, this kind of realistic perspective can facilitate a natural kind of humility as opposed to the forced attempt at a virtue commanded by an authoritative source. And that means it's a kind of humility that allows self-esteem and says it's okay to feel proud of a job well done.

I say yes to aiming for this kind of humility.

Regardless of how you arrive at humility, one of its benefits is an openness to new ideas. Humble people are better at admitting what they don't know, and that awareness can enhance a thirst for new information, insights, and relationships.

The opposite of an open mind is a closed one. Close-minded people build rooms with no windows. Close-minded people fear how new ideas will affect their self-esteem and their ways of coping with life.

Close-minded people tend to be arrogant. Arrogance says things like, "Of course I'm right" and "You don't know what you're talking about."

Arrogance is unattractive. Arrogance is a wall.

Humility is admirable. Humility is an open door.

I vote for humility, but don't ask me if I'm humble. Ask me if I'm working to keep a good perspective on who I am in the whole scheme of things.

Core Value

Humility: Humility is the opposite of arrogance, and it's about keeping your perspective on who you are in the whole scheme of things.

Gratitude

One of the most natural expressions of humility is gratitude. Gratitude is a way of acknowledging that you are not the source of everything good in your life.

After I left my faith, I remembered something I read when I was a minister: "Thanksgiving is the hardest holiday for non-believers because they have no one to thank." It was a put-down, a taunt to non-believers, and I used it in a Thanksgiving sermon after reading it. Decades later, my rejection of faith put me on the receiving end of this condescending jab, but I decided that was okay.

Admittedly, gratitude for life and all the good it brings is harder to aim without a personal deity to thank, but that doesn't mean a secular-minded individual can't be grateful.

I'm grateful to be alive, and I'm extremely thankful for the good things about life that I can't really thank other people for, things like: the beauty of a sunny day, the cozy melancholy of a rainy afternoon, the drama of a lightning storm, the wonder of the Grand Canyon, the grace of the birds that fly over the small lake behind my house, and so many, many other things. I feel grateful for all these "gifts" without needing to identify a specific source for them.

The same is true of my gratitude for the good fortune of having family and friends, my thankfulness for the positive things that happen in my life, and my sense of—for lack of a more secular expression—being richly blessed. My level of gratitude is not hindered at all by the lack of a personal God to thank.

In my Christian life, I felt obligated to be grateful. The Bible commanded me to be thankful, and sometimes, I felt that I could never be thankful enough. Sometimes I felt guilty that I was not more grateful.

I no longer practice gratitude in obedience to directives from the Bible. Any thankful attitude that I now hold is not an obligation. It's a natural response, a voluntary feeling, and I like that.

I don't pray anymore, but I can freely choose to be silent for a few moments to think about things for which I am thankful. I can journal about what I appreciate. I can pause before eating to feel grateful. And of course, gratitude includes expressing appreciation to other people.

Saying "thank you" is such a basic part of our interactions with others. What kind of people don't say thank you: bullies and other rude people, self-centered people, and people who lack social awareness. An instantly understandable put-down of another person is to say he or

Gratitude

she is an ingrate.

If you give something to a small child and a parent is present, you can assume the parent will quickly remind the child to say thank you. It's fundamental human training.

Gratitude is about treating others the way we would like to be treated. Who doesn't like it when someone else shows their appreciation?

We walk down the path of meaning when we become creatively articulate in our expressions of gratitude to other people. A phone call just to say thank you, a special gift, an intense look in the eye when verbally thanking someone—all have the potential to become memorable moments that are good for the giver of gratitude and the recipient.

Virtually every book or article I've read about how to be happy includes gratitude as one of the ingredients. Being grateful is a good way to live.

Core Value

Gratitude: Remember that you are not the source of everything that is valuable in your life and make a habit of being grateful for all the good that comes your way.

Generosity

According to the Gospels of the New Testament, Jesus taught his followers to go the extra mile—to give more than what was commonly expected—to go beyond reciprocity.

In my decades of service as a minister, I saw many Christians going the extra mile, giving more than they received, and attempting to display a servant attitude toward others—just as Jesus taught. To keep things in perspective, these same Christians believed God would reward them for their faithfulness.

Believers see faith in Jesus as the pathway to heaven, but the validity of one's faith is shown by actions. And acts of goodness—like generous sharing of time, talents, and money—are expected to be a VIP badge of honor for believers in the life to come.

If you are a follower of Jesus, you have a clear directive to go the extra mile and the anticipation of eternal benefits for doing so. But for people like me who believe no personal God is evaluating our lives, it makes sense to ask: Is there any reason to go the extra mile—to step beyond reciprocity—ever? Is there any reason to be generous or to give to people who have nothing to give back? Does giving more than you receive make sense when there is no afterlife—no ultimate balancing of the scales where you will be eternally honored for the times you gave more than you got?

I say yes. Generosity makes sense even when you don't believe in God or an afterlife.

Think of the concept of going the extra mile as it applies to relationships. For instance, which do you think works better in a marriage—a relationship in which each partner is careful to give 50 percent but no more, or a relationship in which each partner gives 110 percent? If you're not sure of the answer, ask two or three couples in long-term, successful relationships what they think.

The same is true in just about any kind of relationship, whether it is a friendship or a business connection. Going the extra mile is not only admirable, but it feels good and frequently yields unexpected benefits in a multitude of ways.

I think it's telling that even people who are not generous themselves frequently admire people who are. And I believe this grows out of an instinctive recognition that giving more than you get is life on a higher plane.

When I was a small child, one of my aunts gave me two pennies to buy two pieces of round chewing gum from a vending machine full of multi-colored gumballs. I placed the first penny in the slot, pushed the lever to the left until

Generosity

the machine clicked, and out rolled a red gumball, making a metallic sound when it hit the little swinging door that kept it from falling onto the floor.

As I opened the door, pulled out the gumball, and put it in my mouth, I noticed a boy, slightly younger than me, standing nearby. He was looking longingly at me and at the gumball machine.

I placed my second penny in the slot, pulled the lever, and gave him the second gumball. The expression on his face had helped me decide I didn't need two gumballs to chew.

I'll never forget what transpired next. My aunt, observing what happened, grabbed me by the arm and pulled me aside. She was disappointed and upset. She bent down to look me right in the face as she admonished me: "No, no, don't do that. Be stingy!"

I'm sure I was no more than four or five years old, but I remember thinking that my aunt didn't know what she was talking about. I silently rejected her admonition and felt good about giving my second piece of gum to the boy.

It seemed like a no-brainer to me: Sharing is a good thing to do. Maybe I learned it in Sunday School. Maybe I learned it from my dad—one of his cousins told me that my father was the kind of guy who would give you the shirt off his back. Or maybe it was just something that children intuitively understand before they learn to fear not having enough.

My feelings about generosity haven't changed. And I think sincere generosity conveys a certain confidence, a victory over the fear of not having enough—an anxiety that I'd better hold on to everything I have, or I might end up with nothing.

Giving without expectation of a reward or return seems like a noble thing to do. Even without a divine reference point, it seems right and good—a natural expression of optimism, gratitude, and humility.

I've heard self-made individuals refer to someone less successful and say, "I worked my way up the ladder, and they could too if they tried." But I don't think life always falls so neatly into place.

Imagine a child born to two emotionally sound, physically healthy, well-educated, financially-secure parents. This child comes into the world with good health, a high IQ, a likable disposition, a lean body type, and an attractive face. The child is multi-talented, athletic, energetic, has leadership abilities, enjoys people, and is highly optimistic. And all these traits are apparent by the time the child is five years old.

Now imagine another child born to a single mom who did not finish high school and became a mother at the age of 15. This mom was abused as a child, lives on welfare, is diabetic, and her IQ is 100. This mom suffers from chronic depression, has low self-esteem, and no one, not even her mother, ever told her she was special in any way.

Generosity

It's true that either child could turn out to be a smashing success or a colossal failure by any one of several standards of measurement. Some individuals squander great opportunities, while others overcome tremendous odds. It happens all the time. But it's also true that life will likely be much more challenging for the child born to the single mother on welfare than for the child born into the affluent, healthy, two-parent family.

The point is that we don't all begin life at the same starting line. Some of us have a head start, while others are going to have to work very hard—probably requiring lots of help along the way—just to get to the point where others begin.

When we have a good sense of our place in the big scheme of things, when we realize that we don't all launch from the same starting line, and when we understand how fortunate we are for the starting point we were assigned, generosity is a natural choice. It's an expression of humility, and it's a way of showing gratitude for the good that has come our way—not just by way of our own efforts but also from the luck of the draw.

As a Christian, I was challenged to give sacrificially to support God's work, and I was challenged to go the extra mile for other people. These exhortations came with a promise that there would be honor in heaven for living this way.

Now, there is no invisible God whose work I feel an obligation to support through generous giving and service.

And what I choose to do for others is up to me. This feels like freedom, but it requires setting my own guidelines for living generously.

Generosity will often need the test of balance, especially in ongoing relationships. If I consistently find myself in relationships (or organizations) in which I am always giving, but not receiving much in return, I need to examine why this is the case. I will also need to check my boundaries. A simple boundary is contained in the following response to a request to help, rescue, or volunteer: "No, I'm sorry; that's not something I can do right now." Notice the response begins with the word "no."

Some people and some organizations operate like vacuum cleaners that will suck the emotional life out of you if you let them. Setting boundaries on how often you see or talk to toxic people and setting boundaries on your involvement with any organization that won't stop asking you to give more and more is a good thing.

If a vitality-draining person is a family member or some other irreplaceable person in your life, the challenge is how to maintain a meaningful bond while setting boundaries that allow you to be the whole person you seek to be. For other relationships, discontinuing toxic connections may be the best option. And involvement in an energy-draining organization needs to be evaluated in the same manner as with an energy-draining individual.

Here's another checkpoint: If you are willing to give, but

not willing to receive, that's a warning light for control issues. If you're always on the giving end, there's a reciprocity imbalance, and you have the power—the recipient is likely to feel some uneasy form of obligation to you. If giving is easy but receiving is difficult, figure out why, and aim for the balanced state of giving *and* receiving.

The other side of the equation is that sometimes we may not give enough. If you constantly find yourself in relationships and organizations where you are receiving but giving little or nothing back, self-analysis is in order. Is there a part of you that is afraid to let go, to give generously, and to trust the results? Have you unconsciously—somewhere along the way—become comfortable with being a taker and not a giver?

In a religious environment, you will likely be commanded to be generous. Post faith, I still believe generosity is an important core value and a good way to live, but I think it works better when it's something you freely choose to do.

Core Value

Generosity: Practice a generosity that flows from a positive, confident attitude. It's an admirable way to live. But remember that you get to decide how generous you want to be.

Love

Y ou don't have to love someone if you don't want to. If your response is, "Everybody knows that," you've probably never been religious.[1]

I lived 50 years of my life committed to my Christian faith. The number one commandment—made clear in words attributed to Jesus—is to love God with all your heart, soul, mind, and strength.[4] I now see this as an impossible goal, but it's what I tried to do. Over those years, I expressed my love for God by attempting to follow the ethical guidelines of my faith, by studying to learn more and more about God, and by faithfully attending church.

My love of God was in response to what I believed was his love for me. I saw him as my creator, my loving heavenly father. And, he sent his only son—who was both separate from him and the same as him—to die for my sins.

My sense of a call to ministry at the age of 16 was a response to the call of a loving God, and it was a

---

[1] In the Introduction, I indicated that what I have to say in this book can make sense and work not just for non-believers like me, but for people of faith as well. This chapter may be one of a few exceptions to that guarantee. But keep reading. You may be surprised.

commitment to spend my life sharing God's love with other people.

For decades, I worshipped God, I served God, and I prayed to God—and the basis for all of it was showing my love for the God who loved me first.

Christians are commanded not to worship idols—human-made sculptures that represent a deity—and it was easy to preach about the foolishness of primitive religions in which people pray to a silent statue made of stone.

In the end, for me, relating to the God of my faith wasn't much different from talking to a stone god. How can you be in a loving relationship with an invisible, silent being you've only read about in a book? I realize these words are likely offensive to you if you are a follower of Jesus. I'm torn between truth-telling and kindness here. But I'm sharing my experience. I recognize that your experience may be different.

When I was a believer, participating in religious services with other Christians, and in my case, leading such services, did generate a sense that something was there, something we could all feel.

A congregation of devoted believers singing heartfelt songs of faith made what we all believed seem more real, more present, and more palpable. I remember one song often sung as a solo in church, and it repeated—over and over the words: "My God is real. My God is real." We

Love

didn't need songs that said, "My spouse is real" or "My car is real." But we did need a song that said, "My God is real," because none of us could see or hear God in any normal way. We needed to get together and stir ourselves up with song and sermon to stoke the fire of our faith.

If you're not a person of faith, you're probably only minutes away from someone who will assure you that "My God is real, and I feel his presence in my life every day." I understand that sense of faith, but I also know that whoever makes such a statement has never heard the voice of God in a way that moves an eardrum and has never seen God in a way a camera could record.

When I left my faith, one of the ways in which I felt a sense of relief was in no longer needing to pretend to be in a loving relationship with a God who is silent and invisible.

The Christian faith teaches children and adults to love someone they can't see whether they want to love him or not. And if you don't love the invisible God, you're in trouble. It's crazy thinking: "Love God as he loves you, or you will be punished!"

You might be thinking, "I understand your argument that you don't have to love a God who isn't there, but what about love for other people? Why isn't the imperative of loving other people the first item in this list of core values?" That's a valid question that deserves an answer.

Putting love last in my list of core values is a reaction to being commanded to love for most of my life, then realizing that neither I nor anyone else is capable of loving everyone, and finally deciding I get to choose who I love. However, placing love last on my list is about more than that.

I can't visualize any kind of meaningful life that is devoid of loving relationships, but I don't want to overuse and cheapen the concept of loving others. And I have come to believe that in much the same way that humility is best attained by focusing on something other than humility, love for others is likely to happen more naturally when we focus on the things that create and energize good relationships.

Think of it this way: Follow the relationship guidelines suggested in the preceding pages. Practice the core values of strength, kindness, truthfulness, humility, gratitude, and generosity in relationships. Then see when, where, and with whom love happens. My money is on love being the fruit of meaningful human connections that grow out of the practice of these guidelines and values.

So, instead of imploring you to love, I implore you to be kind—and kindness includes respect, empathy, patience, and forgiveness. I commend the value of truthfulness that is delivered with kindness. I encourage you to find the strength and courage to keep your commitments, live by your values, and overcome your fears. Choose humility. Practice gratitude. Be generous. And let love happen naturally. Can you imagine a person who lives these values not being a loving person? I can't.

I love the idea of love happening not as the result of an imperative, but rather as the natural consequence of who we are and the natural outcome of the values we practice.

This is a liberating concept: You don't have to love someone if you don't want to. My old religious self gives me a jab when I write those words, but I'm going to ignore the jab and stick with the concept: You don't have to love someone if you don't want to.

I'm assuming there are and will be people you want to love. Being emotional-intimacy-capable is required if you want to be able to give and receive love at the deepest level. Establishing boundaries and reminding yourself that you always have the right to say how much you want to trust and how far you want to go in a relationship are relational tools that promote a feeling of safety and a sense that interactions are not out of control.

If you've been hurt deeply in the past, love can be frightening—so much so that when someone moves a step closer to you in a friendship or a romantic relationship, you may instinctively take a step in the other direction. This is ultimately a self-destructive response, and it behooves you to get whatever help is needed to figure out why it is happening and what you need to do to change it.

Because I hope for you to live the most meaningful life possible, it is also my wish that your life will be full of love, not only toward others, but from a wide array of diverse individuals who recognize your uniqueness, your contributions, and your value in this world.

Core Value

Love: Let love happen naturally. You don't have to love someone if you don't want to. Just remember to be kind to everyone as much as humanly possible. And when love happens, don't be frightened by it and run away.

Purpose

Religious people are taught to find meaning and purpose in reference to God, his promises, and his plan for their lives. Secular people find their own meaning by discovering and following a value-driven purpose without reference to God or religion.

Given the distinction between religious and secular people described above, you might be tempted to skip this chapter if you're a person of faith. That would be a mistake in my view. Although your religion—by its very nature—dictates many of your overarching goals, you are still tasked with determining your own distinctive role in life.

So, regardless of where you stand on the spectrum of belief versus non-belief, I challenge you to recognize the importance of discovering and articulating your unique purpose.

Clearly defining your purpose can be a meaningful process even if you're already on a chosen path and feel that you currently have a good sense of what your purpose is.

You can start your purpose search immediately by making three lists on a piece of paper: your core values, your talents, and a list of things you are passionate about. As you review your lists, if you see an item in one list that has some logical connection with an item in another list, draw a connecting line between them. Look for as many connections as you can find. Take your time. Working on these lists over a period of several days is a good strategy.

Next, with your three lists and their connected items in mind, pretend you're looking back on your life in later years and describing the one thing that has obviously been your purpose. Write one or two sentences to describe this one thing. What you write may or may not be about your vocation, but it needs to be about what matters most to you in terms of purpose. Take several days to mull over what you've written. Keep thinking about what matters most to you. Rewrite or polish your life description statement until you feel it is just right.

Once you feel good about your purpose statement, start thinking—on a daily basis—of what you've written as your actual life purpose. Think of your life purpose declaration as if it were a new article of clothing. How does it fit? Is it comfortable? Are you happy to own it?

Do any new activities, studies, trips, talks, or other life events happen naturally as you pursue your newly stated purpose? How do you feel about these new experiences?

After trying out the purpose statement you've adopted for a few days or weeks, if you don't feel good about it, that's okay. Start over and try again. Take your time and be patient with yourself, but don't give up.

Purpose

What you're looking for is a sense of purpose, driven by something you're passionate about, something that is in line with your core values. Follow the things that matter most to you, including your talents, passions, and core values, to find your purpose. Then, you can pursue your purpose to find meaning.

A premise of this book is that purpose and meaning are more important than happiness. Our level of happiness will rise and fall with life events. And sometimes, happiness is not appropriate for what is happening in our lives. Sometimes we need to struggle. Sometimes we need to grieve. Some days will feel better than others. But even when we are experiencing a shortage of reasons to feel happy, we can seek to be fully engaged in doing what feels fulfilling.

The positive psychology movement has given us the concept of flow, which refers to the sense of being so involved in what you are doing that you become unaware of the passing of time. When you are in this state of energized focus, you are likely to look up and say, "I can't believe two hours have passed." We have more control over creating and experiencing flow than we do over feeling happy.

Happy is wonderful. I hope for as much of it as I can get, and I believe in having a positive attitude. However, if my own happiness is all I seek, I will often fail, and I will frequently feel empty. I choose instead to focus on what energizes me.

Before writing this book, I worked with a life coach to make a course correction for a new stage in my life. I wanted to reflect on the work I was doing. I wanted to review my core values. I wanted to be sure I was following my passion, and I wanted to reassess my purpose. The result: I determined that my purpose for my current season of life is helping others find insights that lead to personal growth.

Writing this book is tied to my updated sense of purpose. Writing these words feels meaningful. Sometimes, writing is exasperating, but most of the time when writing, I feel a sense of flow—an energized focus. Time passes quickly. I'm likely to continue until I just can't write any more or until some other important task demands my attention.

Working on tasks that flow out of my purpose has a smooth feeling about it. When you follow your passion, a self-propelled energy is involved. That doesn't mean it's never frustrating or discouraging, but it does mean that—most of the time—it feels good when you're doing it. And when it doesn't feel good, it's still worth the effort.

If you can link your passion to your work, you're extremely fortunate. If that's not possible, find ways to weave what you are most passionate about into the fabric of your daily life. And if it's not possible to get paid for what you're passionate about right now, maybe you could develop a plan and a path to get you to that place at a later date.

Purpose

Time flies when you're having fun, but time also flies when you are living out what you have discovered to be a meaningful, value-driven purpose for yourself, something you are passionate about, something that makes life flow.

Life Principle

Purpose Matters: Meaning comes from pursuing a value-driven purpose you are passionate about. Find and follow your own unique purpose in life.

Expectancy

Phrases like the daily grind, the nine-to-five routine, and the treadmill of life complain of a sense of being trapped in an endless, recurring cycle. While it's true we can never escape certain repetitive aspects of life—waking, eating, bio breaks, sleeping, and starting over the next day—we can learn to embrace a larger view.

The grander view is seeing life as a journey—a trek in which one thing is certain—we need to keep moving forward. The alternatives are being stuck in a hamster cage, or worse, moving backwards to an earlier state, sinking into depression, and watching life pass you by.

Some of life's most meaningful moments can happen while you're standing still, sitting down, or when you're flat on your back. But to have a sense of meaning that goes beyond mere moments, a fulfillment that is more consistently present—you need a sense of moving forward.

We can teach ourselves to see life as an exciting expedition, not a straight-line trip from here to there, but rather, an exploratory journey with countless stops, side trips, and multiple course corrections along the way.

Sometimes our destinations will be planned targets on our route—places we've worked long and hard to reach. But we'll also discover lovely spots we didn't know existed—surprising places that demand more than a moment's attention to soak in all they have to offer. And sometimes we'll need to stop for repairs.

The fuel for forward movement on this journey is a sense of expectancy—the idea that no matter how difficult or great life has been so far, something worth looking forward to lies ahead. That something good could be the result of completing a project you're working on, or it could be some out-of-the-blue, wonderful thing you never anticipated. Expectancy is a readiness for a new idea, event, or person that will lead to unexpected enlightenment, growth, or joy.

Believing the best is yet to come is natural when you believe in life after death, but looking for eternity can be a way to miss the value of the here and now. I no longer expect an existence beyond this one, but I still choose to believe the best is yet to come in the one life that I know is real.

Advocating a sense of expectancy is another way of saying, "Don't give up on hope."

I want to be careful that this does not come across as a callous disregard for anyone whose life feels hopeless. Sometimes we can feel like we're drowning, and in such times we need help from someone who's in a better place.

Expectancy

If you've never needed someone to throw you a life preserver, consider yourself extremely fortunate, and I suggest humility because your status could change in an instant.

If you're in a place where the possibility of good things ahead seems like a foolish fantasy, regardless of how bad things may be, I still say, "Don't give in to hopelessness." I know it's easy for me to say, and I know life is not always fair. But I also know that if any one of us gives in to hopelessness, we can sink so deep into the darkness of despair that we may not see the outstretched hand of opportunity when it is offered.

My Christian belief system told me that no matter what happened, no matter how bad it seemed, I could trust that God was working through the negative events in my life for my greater good. Maybe that's how you still cope with tough times. It's different for me now. Since I no longer rely on what I once viewed as promises from God, I don't have any assurances that good things lie ahead for me. It may not be logical, but I still choose to expect good things to happen. I take this view because having a positive attitude about the future makes me ready to see and participate when good does come my way. But I also take this view because it prompts me to work to make good things happen.

I understand that bad things can happen to me with no good elements in or around them. But no matter what happens, one thing that is virtually impossible to take from me is the decision to look ahead with hopeful expectancy.

In my life beyond faith, hopeful expectancy is the closest thing I have to faith, and I choose to let this expectancy gently pull me forward in my journey.

I invite you to join me in choosing to believe that something good lies ahead.

Life Principle

Expectancy Matters: Choose to believe that something good lies ahead. You're more likely not to miss something good when you're looking for it.

Pacing

If you view life as a journey and you believe something good lies ahead, it makes sense to keep moving forward. One key to continued forward movement in life is not running yourself into the ground, and the way to avoid burning out is to pace yourself.

> But they that wait upon the Lord shall renew their strength; they shall mount up with wings as eagles; they shall run, and not be weary; and they shall walk, and not faint. Isaiah 40:31

Yes, I just quoted a verse from the King James Bible, but I haven't reverted to preaching. It's still the secular me addressing you, and I'm not advocating waiting on God. Sometimes Bible verses communicate truths that transcend its supernatural message. Isaiah 40:31 is a good example as it describes four states regarding movement—stationary (waiting), walking, running, and flying. These four travel states provide a good model for our *moving forward in life* metaphor, and they remind us that pacing matters.

I would not want to run through an art exhibit. I don't need a jet to get to the grocery store. I wouldn't want to try to walk from Texas to Canada. And if I'm in a foot race, I don't want to be standing still. In other words, different modes and speeds are appropriate for different situations.

When you experience a great loss in your life—a death, a divorce, a career failure, or any other severe cause of grief, you'll need to sit for a while. You'll need to stop to regain your bearing. You'll need to pause to feel your emotions. These are healthy things to do—normal when working through a loss.

Then, as the shock and numbness wear off, you'll be accomplishing a lot to get out of bed each day and do the normal things you need to do. You'll be in a walking mode. When you've experienced a major setback, and you're just getting back into your routine, it's an accomplishment to keep putting one foot in front of the other.

Eventually, with enough time and enough processing of your grief, all options for forward movement will be back on the table.

Sometimes, you'll be in a running mode. You're working toward a goal. You're excited about it. You're pushing hard, and all the lights are green. Run, run, run! The finish line looks good!

Every now and then, if you're lucky, you'll feel like you're flying—a child is born, one of your dreams comes true, or something happens that exceeds your wildest expectations.

Pacing

Soaring feels good.

Sometimes we crash. We aim too high, and we fall. We run too far, and we collapse in exhaustion. These are times when life is telling us we must stop and recharge.

We need balance in our travel modes. This includes seeing our meaningful "standing still moments" as part of our forward movement. Taking time to stop, to focus on our breathing, to meditate, to practice mindfulness—these are travel skills.

Mindful waiting is part of the desired pace for living. This waiting is about having patience—not needing to have everything make itself clear, happen, unfold, or gain closure right now. It's about learning to trust the process of planting seeds and letting them grow. It's about sitting quietly, listening to your breathing, and finding peace in the moment.

We each have our own kind of inertia. Some of us have trouble getting started while others have a hard time standing still. Some of us need a little heat under the seat to get us going, and some of us need help in slowing down. Our challenges at pacing will be different depending on what our inherent inertia state looks like.

Life Principle

Pacing Matters: Pace yourself in life's journey—walking, being still, running, and flying—all have their place.

Now

Having a hopeful sense of expectancy is a crucial mindset for approaching the future, but it's not the only important aspect of looking ahead. Visualizing how you would like your life to look in the future is a step toward improving, growing, and moving forward. Planning is a way of taking responsibility for your life, whether it's thinking about a job change, scheduling a vacation, or buying an insurance policy. It's hard to see how anyone could live a meaningful life without spending some time looking ahead.

And there are times when we need to focus on the past. It's hard to learn from the past if you don't reflect on it. If there's pain in your past, embracing that pain is a step toward letting it go—and that involves thinking about the events that created the pain. When we lose a loved one, part of the grief process is remembering. And telling children and grandchildren stories from the past is a way of passing along the wisdom we have acquired.

Looking ahead and looking back are requirements for meaningful living. But it's even more important to recognize that where you are right now—this moment—is the most important place you will ever be, because NOW—not yesterday or tomorrow—is when life happens.

We can miss out on life by focusing too much on regretting past events or worrying too much about what might happen in the future. And even when we're not thinking about the past or the future, we can still be "somewhere else" in the present moment. There are a million ways to be "miles away" while in the presence of an important event or personal interaction.

Since now is when life happens, it's important to be fully engaged in the current moment, to live—as much as possible—in the present tense. As with the options for being "somewhere else," there are countless ways to engage with the present moment, and some of those pathways deserve special attention.

CPR Experiences

Living in the present tense is mainly about a mindset, but there are some types of experiences that demand our present-tense participation—I call them *conscious participation required* experiences.

When a *conscious participation required* experience is in progress, it's virtually impossible to be somewhere else mentally. These are experiences that pull you into the present moment and have a way of resuscitating you when you've fallen into a rut of disengaged living. I like to think of them as CPR experiences.

Some examples of CPR experiences are laughter, play, beauty, wonderment, and connectedness.

A simple self-check for how often you are showing up for the present moment is reviewing the last few days, weeks, or months for the presence—and recurrence—of moments of laughter, play, appreciating beauty, wonderment, meaningful connections, and other *conscious participation required* experiences.

Here's a quick review of these five kinds of CPR experience with some suggestions for putting them into practice right now.

Laughter

Sneezing and laughter are both spontaneous physical events that are hard to stop once they start. Sneezes are cleaning-out events. The purposes of laughter are harder to define, but one thing is certain—laughter is a *conscious participation required* experience.

The importance of laughter is evidenced by the fact that great comedians are paid large sums of money to make us laugh, while—at least as far as I know—no one gets paid to make us sneeze.

Laughter can take on a dark side when it is derisive and mocking, but most of the time, laughter is a positive event.

Do you laugh often? How long has it been since your last belly laugh? How long since you couldn't stop laughing? What are your dependable sources for generating laughter? Are you too serious too much of the time?

Suggestion: If you were in a contest to determine how quickly you could find something that makes you laugh out loud, what would you do? How about actually doing whatever that is by pausing and finding something that will make you laugh in the next few minutes?

Play

Children play; animals play, and adults should play too. We pay to watch others play with skill—football, basketball, baseball, soccer, and more. But we should engage in our own play, the kind where skill doesn't matter and winning isn't necessarily the objective.

There are a million ways to play. Playing is doing something that feels good but doesn't necessarily have a purpose—other than playing. It's a way of disconnecting from life's routine and engaging with the present moment. It's a way of acknowledging there's more to life than winning, working, eating, and sleeping.

Play bridges barriers: age, ethnicity, gender, and sometimes even species.

Suggestion: When was the last time you played just for the sake of play? What if you grabbed your calendar right now and penciled in a time to play?

Beauty

In the philosophy of religion, the existence of beauty is argued to be one of the proofs that God exists. But it doesn't require an attitude of faith to grasp that an ability to conceive of anything as beautiful points to a hard-to-define and somewhat mysterious part of life.

Beauty gets your attention, pulls you toward it, and draws you into the now. Conscious participation is required.

We are enthralled and uplifted by beautiful scenery, paintings, music, and other forms of art. We can't help but notice beautiful people, and we are likely to be biased in their favor, at least initially, even if we're a bit jealous.

There's something about beauty that we all understand. When someone describes an experience as a "beautiful moment," we may have questions as to exactly what happened, but we understand that something wonderful has occurred.

Life without beauty is life in survival mode.

Suggestion: Think of one thing you can do to ensure one or more meaningful interactions with beauty over the next few days? What would it take to make this happen? Why not make it happen?

Wonderment

A sense of wonderment is part of what we often feel in the presence of beauty, but wonderment is about more than beauty. It's about how we respond to the magnitude and mystery of life. Whatever the source—a starry night, a spectacular view, a rocket pushing into space, a newborn baby—when you are experiencing wonderment, you are in the present moment. This is the opposite of a ho-hum approach to life. It is about cultivating an attitude that is on the lookout for anything that evokes a sense of wonder.

When I left my faith, I didn't lose my sense of wonderment—in fact, my capacity for wonder grew. My old approach was pretty much, "Isn't God great." After leaving faith, I began to read and learn more about physics and astronomy. As my understanding of these fields of study grew, so did my capability to experience wonderment at the magnificent complexity of existence. I also became more aware of how much I do not and cannot know, which added to my sense of wonderment.

Suggestion: If it's dark right now and your sky is clear, you could step outside and look at the stars. If that's not possible, you could Google "photos from space" and select the images option. You'll find more than one photo that generates wonderment.

Connectedness

Connectedness occurs when you engage in a meaningful way with a person, group, experience, or event. When you are distracted, disengaged, or isolated, that's the opposite of connectedness.

Connectedness is a vital sign of an emotionally rich, fully engaged life.

When I play with one of my grandchildren, I am connected.

If I hike a wilderness trail with a friend and we enjoy the beauty of nature together, we are connected.

When you take in an eloquent work of art in a museum, you are likely connected to its beauty, its message, and to some aspect of it that is hard to describe.

When you look at the moon in awe and wonder, you're connected to the mystery of our existence.

When you sit in an audience enthralled by an inspirational speaker, you're connected with the speaker, other members of the audience, and with a vision of something uplifting.

When you are having an open, honest conversation with another person, you are connected not just by the words being spoken, but also by the emotional intimacy of the moment.

There is an aspect of connecting in each of these ways that allows us to feel we are part of something outside of and beyond ourselves. And when we are connected, we are in the present moment.

Suggestion: Call one of your best friends and tell them three things you appreciate about them. A significant, connected moment is likely to happen.

Vital Signs

Conscious participation required experiences are vital

signs of an emotionally rich, fully-engaged, present tense life. They're harder to find when you're depressed or under the control of fear. They will slip away when you're moving too fast to smell the roses.

When you feel like you are dying emotionally, when you are dabbling with despair, when dread is haunting you, when each hour feels way too much like the one before, look for a CPR experience. Look for the resuscitation of laughter, play, beauty, wonderment, and connectedness.

Conscious participation required experiences are but one way to be in the now moment. Keep in mind that living in the present tense is mainly about a mindset. It's about finding the balance of learning from the past and planning for the future while focusing on capturing the fullness of the present moment.

Life Principle

Now Matters: Cultivate a mindset of living in the present tense, checking periodically for recurring *conscious participation required* experiences like laughter, play, beauty, and wonderment.

Relationships

We humans have evolved to need connections with other people. For any one of us, death would not be far behind our abandonment to some cold, isolated, wilderness spot with no shelter, medicine, or human help. We need each other to survive in this world.

I depend on other people for clean water and nutritious food. I've never built a house, a car, or a highway, but I need all three. I require the help of others to power my home and make gasoline for my car. From time to time, I need the help of a doctor, and I'm glad there are multiple emergency care centers near my home. I'm not alone in these dependencies. We all count on other people to stay alive.

We humans do not have the ferociousness of a lion or the strength of a gorilla. But we do have large brains, and one thing we learned long, long ago is that we need each other. We've learned to survive by cooperating, sharing resources, and working together.

You don't have to be on a search for meaning to recognize the importance of transactional connections with other people—exchanges for food, clothing, shelter, transportation, and other necessities of life. But aiming for the highest and best in life requires a desire for and a willingness to engage in more than bartering with other people.

Whether we're introverted or extroverted, isn't a life filled with positive relationships what we all desire?

Imagine a scientist who virtually lives in a lab—working almost every waking hour, seldom coming up for air, and going home alone each night. Then, after decades of hard work, this medical researcher finds a cure for cancer and dies shortly after making the historic discovery. No one could describe such a life as a meaningless one, but it would be hard to think of it as an enviable life.

You might perform well in some jobs without people skills and positive relationships, but you can't be good at life if relationship tools are absent and you are living in isolation.

Here are a few suggestions for building and maintaining meaningful relationships with other people.

Value Each Relationship for What It Is

For much of my adult life, my expectations were extremely high for every new friendship I made. I was ready to give of myself, and I wanted all my friends to be best friends. I was often disappointed. A light bulb moment occurred when a wise counselor challenged me to view each friendship, whether new or old, with a willingness to value it for whatever it could provide—a glass half-full rather than half-empty approach.

If a friendship touched only one part of my life or the depth of conversations was not all I desired, I could choose to see that relationship as having value for what it did provide, rather than rejecting or minimizing it because of what it did not deliver. I could be grateful for what each friend was able to share.

This was a liberating concept for me: *Don't expect every friendship to be the greatest you'll ever have—lighten up and be grateful for any human connection.* It was liberating because it got me in sync with reality: Some relationships have more potential for depth, trust, longevity, and meaning than others. Small talk is not always a bad thing, and every positive human tie has value.

Accepting this truth did not stop me from placing a priority on seeking deeper relationships. And when I do find someone with whom I can talk honestly about anything, someone who is usually on the same page as me, and even when they're not, somehow, we still connect—that is a serendipitous event for which I am especially grateful. And it's a relationship to be treated as one would guard and protect a precious treasure, something you take care not to lose.

It's also true that not expecting too much too soon in a relationship allows it time to develop. What seems like a shallow connection at first can turn into a deeper one as two individuals learn to trust one another. Time, conversation, and shared events often allow this to happen gradually. Some close relationships hit the ground running, while others take time to grow.

All human connections have value, but high-trust, reliable, this-is-who-I-really-am relationships are priceless. We can increase the likelihood of developing such connections by practicing active listening, transparency, and accountability—and by connecting with one or more communities of like-minded people.

Engage in Active Listening

A basic tool for relationship building is the skill of active listening—a type of listening that looks deeper. This is not a search for embarrassing truths or secret failures. This is about connecting with another person at a more profound level.

Learn to ask questions and to pay attention to the answers. Be curious about who the other person is, what they have to share, what is beneath the surface, and what is unique about their story.

Think of active listening as a multi-sensory experience. Look for body-language cues. What is the emotional tone of the conversation? What is not being said? What facial expressions point to a message between the lines? What emotions do you feel as you listen?

When you practice active listening, you will find that you

frequently walk away from a conversation with someone you've just met knowing much more about him or her than they know about you. But that's okay. What you will also find—eventually—are individuals who can reciprocate your level of interest, and that's how important connections with others can begin and grow.

Be Honest, Open, and Vulnerable

Deeper connections with other people will develop as we cultivate our skills for being honest, open, and vulnerable.

Emotional recklessness is not required. Personal boundaries are important. We're looking for selected safe people who are worthy of our trust, and we need to remember that not everyone is trustworthy.

The first step is being a safe person yourself. Don't violate confidences. Be what you seek in others.

It's a good idea to become vulnerable with another person one step at a time. First, we can infer how someone will keep our confidences by how that individual talks about others. Then, we can share one "low cost" disclosure and watch for indications that our confidentiality is being honored. We can test the waters, so to speak, and allow time and multiple engagements with another person before we trust them fully.

If I share too much, and my confidant breaks our agreement by telling someone else what I've shared, I will let myself feel the pain, learn from the experience, and measure what I say to this person in the future.

Over time, we learn that one friend can be trusted at one level—with some limitations—while another friend can be trusted more. A few are worthy of unlimited trust.

Be cautious of someone who is ready for you to reveal all but shows little or no personal vulnerability themselves. That's a warning sign.

Being honest, open, and vulnerable creates the possibility of emotional intimacy which is the key to a deep relationship of any kind. If you are unable to be honest and open about yourself, if you are so afraid of being hurt that you are totally closed to everyone, you are an island. And it would be beneficial to find, learn about, and address the source of your fear of self-revelation.[5]

Practice Accountability

A key aspect of living a meaningful life is taking responsibility for our actions. Choosing to be accountable in the context of relationships is part of how we make sure that happens.

Being accountable does not mean surrendering your personal boundaries, and it does not mean submitting to the authority of another person who is unopen to feedback from anyone else. We are looking for selected safe people.

We need to find trustworthy, like-minded confidants who will, at our request, lovingly, but honestly, tell us what they see in our actions. They will not limit their feedback to the good they see in us. They will call us to task when we have asked for feedback. and they have seen us violating our own values. They will speak the truth with courage and kindness as we make ourselves accountable to them.

Find Community

Human relationships thrive in the context of warm, supportive, and helpful communities.

If you're a person of faith, the people you worship with may be your most important community. Being a part of a fellowship of faith is something I understand because I made it a priority for most of my life.

Now, as a non-believer, my primary understanding of the world and how it works comes from science. But science does not provide the personal encouragement of a caring community.

Science provides the technology and medicine for healing care in a hospital, but science will not pay a visit, hold your hand, and express personal concern.

The discoveries of science will likely lead to a longer life than any of us would have known otherwise, but when we die, science will not attend the funeral service to eulogize us and say encouraging words to those left behind.

Science can help you better understand what makes people—including yourself—who they are, but it will not offer a communal group that helps you feel loved and accepted. Science—as far as I know—does not provide a weekly meeting where you can be encouraged to keep working on being a better person.

Free-thinking non-believers like me may not be so dependent on a like-minded tribe as those who build their lives around a community of faith, but we too need the benefits provided by one or more caring communities.

Secular communities that meet regularly and mirror some of the same concerns as churches, synagogues, and mosques—but without reference to deity—now exist in some U.S. cities.[6] If you're not a person of faith and live in a city that has one of these groups, visiting one of their meetings could be the start of a meaningful connection for you. You can Google "secular community near me" to see what's available.

If connecting with a local secular group is not an option, you can build your own network of like-minded support people. You can connect across geographical lines, via online, regional, or national groups. Google searches for "humanist groups," "atheist groups," and "agnostic groups" will point to helpful options. You also can find meaningful connections on Facebook and Twitter.

And there's great value in finding even a few friends who see life in a similar way, especially if that's all that's available to you. A group does not have to be large to serve as a caring community. And, even as a secular individual, you may find community with individuals who are religious but are like-minded in other ways that make it possible to connect. Finally, don't forget that family connections strong enough to transcend differences in religious views can be one of your most important forms of community.

Maintain Boundaries

Healthy relationships require boundaries. Boundaries are different than walls. Relational walls keep everyone at bay. Boundaries are protective filters that safeguard us from harmful interactions while permitting safe connections.

If you feel someone is standing too close to you, your physical boundary has been crossed. If someone touches you in a sexual way without permission, your sexual boundaries have been violated. If someone calls you abusive names and walks over your feelings, your emotional boundaries are being breached. And if someone puts you down because your views about God are not the same as theirs, your religious boundaries are being ignored.

If you're in a relationship with someone who constantly violates your boundaries even after you've called them on it multiple times, that's a relationship that needs to be improved, restricted, or possibly, ended.

Boundaries work in two directions. I need to be sure my own boundaries are intact, and I need to enforce them. But

I also need to respect other people's boundaries.

If you were raised in a boundary-respecting environment, it's likely that enforcing your own personal boundaries and honoring the boundaries of other people come naturally. But if you experienced repeated violations of your boundaries in your formative years, you may have become more susceptible to boundary violations by others. You may live with little or no self-protection or you may live in an emotional fortress that keeps others at arms-length. And without realizing it, you may have trouble recognizing and respecting the boundaries of others.

But we are not stuck where we start. We can all learn, build, and improve our boundary skills. Regardless of how easy or hard boundaries are for you, regular self-directed boundary checkups are in order.

Relationships matter—maybe more than anything else—and we can each learn more, build skills, and do the things that create and build healthy, meaningful relationships.

Life Principle

Relationships Matter: Value each relationship for what it is and do the things that enable relationships to grow. Engage in active listening. Be honest, open, and vulnerable. Practice accountability. Connect with a community. Live boundary-sensitive.

Toxicity

Synonyms for the word toxic include: harmful, dangerous, and destructive. This chapter is about four toxic patterns of thinking that are harmful, dangerous, and destructive—psychological burdens that matter because they can tear down self-esteem, damage relationships, and impede our forward progress in life.

Shame

It's helpful to think of guilt as a feeling about things you've done, and shame as a feeling of needing to hide some aspect of who you are. Shame isn't all bad. The ability to feel shame keeps us from walking down the street with no clothes on, and the capacity to feel appropriate shame marks us as civilized. But an ever-present shame that constantly cajoles you to hide some part of who you are is toxic shame. Toxic shame serves no useful purpose. It doesn't show up to make you a better person. Its only aim is to make you feel bad about yourself, and it loves to exaggerate.

Toxic shame can be like a swarm of pesky mosquitos that annoy you only when you stand in the wrong place, or it can be more pervasive. If you were shamed repeatedly in your formative years, or if you took on the shame of a dysfunctional parent who would not own their own shame, you may have emerged from childhood with toxic shame hard-wired into your sense of self—what's called a shame-based identity. It's not an incurable condition, but the symptoms and side-effects can be deadly when not addressed.

Chronic toxic shame may be invisible to everyone but the person who is living in the pain it generates, or it can self-reveal in different ways. In one mode, the shame-based individual says, "I'm sorry" an awful lot, and may seem ready to apologize for even existing. On the other end of the spectrum, a shame-based person may act shamelessly, as if in defiance of a hidden tormenter. Either way, when you're shame-based, you may repeat shaming behavior that was modeled for you, and you may make a habit of blaming others.

Toxic shame is a burden we can reject, but it will take some work if it has been drilled in deep. If you understand all too well the descriptions of toxic shame in the preceding paragraphs and your understanding comes from your own battle with shame, don't hesitate to seek help. Reading a good book about shame could be a good place to start. If you need the help of a support group or therapist to break shame's grip on you, don't hesitate to reach out for assistance.

A simple but powerful tool for coping with toxic shame is the phrase: "I give you back your shame." It's meant to be uttered silently when you're being shamed by someone or something and want to shake it off. Giving others back their shame is a thought process that can become a healing habit.

When I completed my book, *Goodbye Jesus*, and was about to release it for publication, I was completely sure of the assertions I had written on the subject of my disbelief. I was not plagued by a fear that the God of my former Christian faith might be real or that hell might await me as an apostate. And yet, I felt twinges of shame for the book I was about to make public. My parents and all my aunts and uncles were deceased, but I could imagine one of my aunts saying, "What would your mother think? How could she deal with your not being a Christian anymore?"

Toxic shame can sneak up on you in a powerful way, even when you think you've conquered it. That was the case with the twinges of shame I felt about upon publishing a spiritual autobiography that chronicled my walk away from faith. Toxic shame is a raw emotion, and it's not unlike a case of indigestion. It's just shows up, uninvited and unpleasant. The release of my book was an opportunity for me to practice what I teach—to say to my religious past: "I give you back your shame."

Guilt

Healthy guilt is a reminder to correct your mistakes. When you take the appropriate actions after doing something wrong, healthy guilt goes away. Toxic guilt is different. Like toxic shame, it's not solution-oriented. Toxic guilt exists simply to make you feel bad, it likes to hang around, it overstates its case against you, and it offers no beneficial actions you can take to make it go away.

When I was a Christian, I believed Jesus died for my sins. In one sense, this was good news because it meant that all my sins—past, present, and future—were forgiven. In another way that may be hard to understand if you have never lived in this mindset, having received salvation from Jesus was also a reason for constant watchfulness for sin.

Though in one respect completely forgiven, I still needed to be aware of sins going forward, confess them to God, and ask his forgiveness. This was about maintaining my day-by-day connection with God, not about avoiding hell since that was already taken care of.

One of the results of this mindset for me, and for anyone else sincerely committed to a similar version of the Christian faith, was that at any given time, cognizant of our human tendency to err, you had to assume you had committed some sin in the last 24 hours—even if you couldn't remember what it was. This had the potential for making you feel a constant need to confess something to God even if you couldn't remember a specific sin you needed to acknowledge. Ironically, participating in a belief system that focuses on forgiveness can lead to a lot of unnecessary wondering about whether you should be feeling guilty.

Today, sin is no longer a meaningful concept to me. I still care about right and wrong, but I don't have a God who is recording my every mistake. I don't give credence to religious authorities who are cataloging and ranking types of disobedient thoughts and actions. Guilt doesn't have a hold on me like it used to. And looking back, it appears that my faith sometimes contributed to my feeling guilty in a way that was harmful instead of helpful.

I still recognize the value of healthy guilt that calls for corrective actions, and I have a sense of accountability to society, family, co-workers, community members, friends, as well as to myself. When I wrong someone, I need to tell that person I'm sorry. In some cases, I will need to ask for their forgiveness.

The way I see things now, we need to admit our failures, talk about them, and somehow, in the confession of how we've failed, in our willingness to take responsibility, and in our readiness to make amends, we can experience a lifting of the burden of guilt and we can forgive ourselves.

If it's guilt about a serious wrong with a cascading web of negative results, the help of an insightful friend, support group, or therapist—in the role of confessor—may be required.

But if the guilt does not respond to the routine described above, if it's a strain that is habitual, unresponsive, and burrowed in deeply, a different set of actions will be needed. It's not unlike dealing with an infestation of insects hiding somewhere in your home. Where are they? How did they get there? What's it going to take to get rid of them, and what needs to be done to keep them from returning? You can read up on the bugs or you can enlist the help of a professional.

Whether you work through your guilt issues on your own or with a counselor, certain steps will be essential. Processing what happened to create the guilt will be important, as will taking responsibility and making amends. Understanding the dynamics of what happened and how the guilt locked itself in place will be significant. You will do well to determine if something about you is conditioning you to serve as a magnet for guilt. And all the preceding actions will set the stage for a plan to gradually remove the guilty thought patterns from your daily routine.

Going forward, identifying, and avoiding chronic sources of toxic guilt should be a top priority. Check for people, organizations, and mindsets that have a way of contributing to perpetual, unhealthy guilt in your life. What you don't listen to and what you don't think about matter. Step away from the poison.

Fear

A certain amount of fear helps us to stay alive. Being afraid to walk across a freeway blindfolded is a good thing. It's good if you're afraid to see how fast your car can go on a rain-soaked, winding country road in the dark of night. But there is a kind of apprehension that magnifies danger and favors the odds of loss, pain, and death in a manner that spawns a toxic form of fear. The phrase "crippling power of fear" is applicable. Toxic fear can immobilize you.

Imagine this. I place a steel beam, 12 feet long, 24 inches wide, and 12 inches high on a concrete floor. I offer you $1,000 to walk the 12 feet from one end of the beam to the other. Will you take me up on my offer? Of course, you will! It's easy money. After you walk the beam and collect your money, suppose I snap my fingers and, magically, a hole—10 feet wide and three stories deep—appears under the steel beam. It's the same beam, just as wide and just as long, but it straddles a deep pit. Will you go for another $1,000? It's the same beam, and—in one sense—the difficulty of walking across it has not increased, but the consequences of falling have changed. You can surely walk across the beam again—if you do not let fear distract you. But that's easier said than done because fear can make it more likely that what you are worried about will actually happen.

A good starting point in dealing with toxic fear is talking to yourself about what frightens you. "What is it that I am actually afraid of?" "When did this fear start?" "What is making this fear so powerful?" "What can I do to move beyond my fear?"

Look to your inner strength and its partner—courage. Find safe ways of walking toward your fear instead of running away from it. Get help if you need it. Make up your mind that you will do whatever it takes to overcome the crippling power of habitual, toxic fear.

Hatred

We can make a case for hating evil if such hatred

empowers us to combat malevolence in an effective way. We could even call this feeling righteous indignation.

But what about hating people simply because they are not "your kind." What about hatred of people because of skin color, religious preferences, gender, or any other arbitrary descriptor?

What about hatred that is fueled by envy?

What about hating someone just because you don't like them?

And what about hating so much, so often, and so naturally that it becomes accurate to describe it as chronic hatred.

You don't have to live very high on a morality scale to understand that hatred is wrong.

But is it wrong to hate—acutely or chronically—if there is no God, no sin, and no ultimate judgment? The answer is simple: Hatred is wrong whether God is real or not because hatred runs counter to the way we've evolved to need cooperation for survival. You don't need faith or religion to know that hatred is destructive.

Hatred loves your fears.

Hatred is an energy burner.

Hatred is a form of arrogance.

Hatred says no to empathy.

Hatred is toxic.

Look to some better part of yourself. Empathize. Turn in a direction where you can practice kindness and love.

Life is too short to let it be poisoned with hatred or any other dangerous way of thinking like toxic shame, toxic guilt, or toxic fear.

Toxic Thinking Matters: Let go of all forms of toxic thinking. Check for the presence of toxic shame, guilt, fear, and hatred. Get help if you need it.

Danger

Parents, grandparents, and teachers warn children about dangers in life. Don't touch the electrical outlets. Don't play with knives. Don't talk to strangers. Come inside if there's a storm.

After learning not to touch a hot stove, my preschool grandson adopted the warning he received as his all-purpose safety reminder. Whenever I explained something to be careful about—no matter what it was—he would indicate he understood by exclaiming: Hot danger!

It makes sense that caring adults issue all kinds of safety warnings to kids they love because this world is full of hot dangers, but the hazards of life are not limited to children.

In an instant, life can become so dangerous that one's search for meaning becomes temporarily meaningless. You can't pursue a meaningful life if you're dead. We can find meaning even in the face of pain, loss, and suffering, but it makes sense to understand and avoid the hot dangers of life whenever we can.

Recognizing danger matters, and a strategy for recognizing and dealing with danger starts with understanding where it comes from.

When I was an evangelical Christian, I accepted a very simple explanation for the danger, pain, and evil in the world:

> Because of the disobedience of Adam and Eve, the world became a dangerous place where suffering and death are possible.
>
> Every person born after this fall of humanity inherits a nature inclined toward sin and susceptible to temptation. Satan is active in the world—an ongoing spiritual battle is in progress—and evil increases when individuals give in to his temptations.
>
> Human suffering is the result of living in a fallen world where one's own sinful choices and the sinful choices of other people cause pain and loss. The fall in Eden also disrupted the natural order of things, creating an unsafe physical world where natural disasters can occur.

When I abandoned my simplistic belief in the existence of Satan and decisions made in a primordial garden, I was left with a disconcerting void. Why is the world such a dangerous place? Why is there so much suffering? Why do people rob, rape, and murder? Why do people abuse children? Why do some people experience pleasure when they inflict pain upon others?

Even without my Christian belief system, even with my new commitment to find reality through reason, I had to admit that evil is real and ever-present.

Based on 2015 averages, in the next hour or so in the U.S., 10 individuals will be raped, and two people will be murdered,[7] unless of course there's another mass shooting with a military-style weapon instantly ending the lives of multiple innocent people in seconds.

The list of horrific ways people hurt each other goes on and on: child pornography, human trafficking, sex slavery, torture, and genocides. We need locks on our doors, and many would say they need guns for protection. Bank tellers in major cities work behind bullet-proof glass. We protect our credit card numbers and our Social Security numbers because we know that funds and identities can be stolen. We walk through metal detectors before we can board airplanes.

If you watch too much news, you might decide that any feeling of safety is an illusion.

If there is no satanic being waging spiritual warfare against humanity, how do we explain all the ways that humans hurt and kill one another? If we are not stained by the sin of an Adam and Eve, then what makes individuals—even groups of people—do things so terrible, so hateful, and so harmful that we must call their behavior evil?

No simple answer exists. Human behavior is complex, and human actions have multiple, often complicated causes. Sometimes good people do bad things, and a small percentage of people are so malevolent that it's hard to see any good in them.

I don't know all the reasons, and I'm not sure anyone has a full explanation. Nonetheless, here are some non-supernatural causes for humans behaving badly—in no particular order.

Animal Instinct

We are evolved animals. A primitive survival instinct resides just below our conscious thinking. This animal nature can be unleashed when our basic human needs for air, water, food, shelter, or safety are not being met. A part of us is designed to fight to stay alive.

When our very existence is at risk and we feel that our options for survival are limited, any one of us may act like a cornered animal.

On the other end of the spectrum, our baser nature can emerge if we become extremely powerful—with access to wealth and influence or dominance in military conflict. If your moral guidelines are not able to hold the line in these situations, power can go to your head in a way that deadens your capacity for empathy and leads you to act like an alpha male beast.

Some of what we call evil happens when animal instincts

prevail over the more evolved parts of the human brain.

Mental Health

The brains of some individuals don't work properly when it comes to making decisions about appropriate behavior.

In *The Sociopath Next Door*, Martha Stout, a psychologist who spent decades studying sociopaths, writes that about one in 25 people in the U.S. is a sociopath.[8]

A sociopath lacks empathy and remorse. Fear of punishment, not conscience, is the sociopath's motivation for following the rules and laws of society—that is if they follow the rules. They feel entitled and will lie to get what they want. A sociopath can be very charming, but it's an act, and the goal is manipulation and control. A sociopath may be incapable of love, is driven by hostility, and is likely to seek revenge.

A vast quantity of human suffering can be traced to the actions of sociopaths—the more power and influence they wield, the more damage they are likely to do.

Sociopathy is but one example. Only a small percentage of individuals with mental illness commit violent acts, but psychotic episodes, paranoid delusions, affective disorders, delirium, dementia, post-traumatic stress, intermittent explosive disorder, sexual sadism, and antisocial personality disorder can be contributing factors. In addition, human behavior can be dramatically affected by a chemical imbalance in the brain.[9]

As I write these words, two mass shootings have just occurred in the U.S., one in El Paso, Texas, the other in Dayton, Ohio—both horrible reminders of what can happen when a tortured, broken mind explodes in hatred.

There are so many ways a malfunctioning brain can lead to doing harm to others. And, some forms of mental illness drive an individual toward self-harm, including suicide, that triggers a damaging ripple effect, inflicting deep suffering on friends and family members.

Substance Abuse

The misuse of ingested substances causes untold loss, suffering, and death. Some 88,000 people die each year in the U.S. from alcohol-related causes alone, and according to the National Institute of Alcohol Abuse and Alcoholism, in 2015, 15.1 million adults 18 or older had an alcohol use disorder.[10]

Substances like cocaine, methamphetamines, and heroin destroy human lives. Prescription drugs can be misused in deadly ways. The opioid crisis is raging, and no one seems to know how to curb it.

Scan today's news for examples. You won't need to check many of your news feeds to find one more notice of a loss triggered by alcohol or drug abuse.

The damage done by substance abuse is not limited to a driving arrest or a hit in the face or an accident or a gunshot. Relationships can be severely damaged or ended by the emotional injuries inflicted by persistent substance abuse. Relatives who are addicted weigh heavily in the concerns of those who love them—often for a lifetime.

Hurt People

The boss yells at Dad because he lost a big contract. At home, Dad yells at Mom, not really because of anything she did, but because the boss yelled at him. Mom, hurt by Dad's outburst, scolds little Jimmy for some random thing he forgot to do. Jimmy feels hurt, so he gives the family cat a kick off the sofa. When someone is hurt, the pain can cascade down through a network of innocents.

When it's more than a passing emotional wound—when, for example, a child is the direct victim of repeated abuse—the damage is more than an uncomfortable moment. The pain becomes chronic, and there are many ways the hurt may be passed on.

Contrary to conventional wisdom, most abuse victims don't become abusers, but it's easy to pass the pain along in other ways. Later in life, the abuse victim's partner may feel pain in the victim's inability to trust—even when the partner has consistently shown him/herself to be worthy of trust. Family's may be pulled down by the chronic depression of a family member abused long ago, but still hurting. When things feel out of control during childhood, we may develop a need to be in control—of everything—and that's not pleasant for those who intersect our paths.

But sometimes childhood abuse is like the mythical

vampire bite where the victim becomes the predator who then inflicts the wound on someone else. And childhood abuse can lead to acting out in other ways besides perpetuating the abuse received early in life. One study indicates that the U.S. prison population has about twice the number of victims of child abuse as compared to the general population.[11]

A similar scenario can take place on a societal level. One nation starts a war. The other side doesn't want combat but must protect itself, so it fights back. Soldiers on the defensive side are primed to inflict additional pain and suffering on their attackers when they see fellow soldiers killed, injured, or find that torture has occurred. What follows is death on both sides—including non-combatants, adults, and children—so-called collateral damage.

Hurt people, because of their own pain, often—in many different ways—hurt other people. And all these actions add up to become part of the sum of pain, suffering, and evil in the world.

Flawed Leadership

Human behavior is affected by the moral quality of human leaders. Leadership affects families, businesses, cities, and nations.

If we are being led by an individual who constantly feels threatened or was severely abused as a child and has not dealt with the impact of that abuse, if we are being led by an active substance abuser, if we are being led by someone who is mentally ill in a way that causes a disconnection with reality, we're in trouble.

And it's not just that seriously flawed leaders lead badly. People who follow flawed leaders sometimes do things they would never consider doing on their own. We have only to consider Scott Peck's example in *People of the Lie*, where he describes how some U.S. soldiers in Vietnam succumbed to a group mentality that sanctioned inhumane treatment of innocent civilians. Individual soldiers committed atrocities they would never have perpetrated on their own—because of bad leadership.[12]

Flawed but charismatic humans in leadership can rally and embolden flawed humans to follow and emulate behaviors driven by fear, selfishness, and greed.

Impersonal Universe

Human beings are not the only cause of terrible events that generate danger, pain, and suffering. Natural disasters like tornadoes, hurricanes, floods, famines, wildfires, and earthquakes touch the lives of millions of people every year.

If you are a multi-millionaire, a rock star, a top professional athlete, or a powerful politician and everything seems to be going your way, it may be easy to think the universe loves you. But if you just lost everything in a flood, or you're not sure you'll ever find a job again, or you're living in an abusive environment, or you're dealing with what seems to be the latest of an endless series of setbacks, the universe may not seem so friendly.

I'm confident that the universe is neither for me nor against me. It doesn't hate or love me. The universe is impersonal and indifferent about what happens to any of us.

The universe operates according to its own natural laws.

If you jump out of a plane without a parachute, you'll find that gravity is uninterested in your well-being—it will do what it does—and pull you down to your death.

If you leap off an ocean liner in the middle of the night hundreds of miles from land, you'll find that the water is not concerned about your survival. If you survive the impact, when you get too tired to swim, the sea will swallow you.

If you hitch a ride on a spacecraft and step outside without a spacesuit, the vacuum of space will be apathetic about your death. It will suck the air out of your lungs and freeze you in an instant.

An impersonal, uncaring universe is the source of many of the destructive, terrifying, and most challenging events we humans must face.

Situational Awareness
So, how do we deal with the fact that human suffering results from bad—sometimes evil—acts by other people and can also be a result of living in an unconcerned

universe that is driven by natural laws?

This question became more acute for me after I stepped away from a life of faith, decided that no personal God is watching over anyone, and determined this life is all I have. Two immediate realizations followed: I may not always be safe, and staying alive is even more important.

You may believe that a loving God is minding the universe and that under his watchful eye, everything happens for a reason. When something dreadful happens in your life, you may say, "In faith, I choose to believe that God will use this terrible event to bring about good in my life." And I assume that as a person of faith, you live with the confident conviction that if some unfortunate event brings your life to an untimely end, a better life awaits you in heaven.

If this is how you see things, I disagree, but I understand and choose not to belittle your choice. After all, this is how I thought for most of my life. But it's not how I think today.

Now, I say everything happens for a million reasons, and nothing guarantees my survival from moment to moment. Sometimes bad things happen, and all we can do is try to survive, and if we do stay alive, we can attempt to learn from what we experienced.

I realize my assertions about an unsympathetic universe may be disturbing—perhaps so unsettling that you cannot allow yourself to believe they might be true. And if that's how you feel, I understand. But I'm attempting to build my views on evidence-based truth, and that's why I see things as I do.

Honestly, I would prefer being able to believe a benevolent deity is watching over me like I used to, but I can't think that way anymore. I cannot unknow what I now understand.

My take on the impersonal nature of the universe does not necessitate despair as the only possible response. My reaction to all the potential for suffering and loss is a decision to practice situational awareness in a dangerous world. And I think that no matter how much you might lean on your faith for comfort and protection, you too understand the need to take care for your own safety. You too understand that it is foolish to practice recklessness.

If we were headed out on an expedition, we would have a sizeable list of preparations to make, and one of the most important would be making sure we were prepared to respond to any danger that might lie ahead. The journey of life is no different. We need to make sure we are prepared to protect ourselves from individuals and groups who would do us harm, and we should not be naïve about the dangers of weather, climate, and the environment.

It makes sense to be informed about danger. It makes sense to find some sense of safety by linking ourselves with people who are kind and good and to join with such people in looking out for one another. And it is admirable when we seek to provide additional help and protection to those among us who are fragile, frail, and especially vulnerable.

Life Principle

Danger Matters: Don't give in to fear but be realistic about life's dangers. Do what you can to protect yourself and others from harm.

Health

It is now my conviction that this life is all I have. The calendar years measured by my birthdays are not preparation for another life that begins when this one ends. When I die, everything is over for me. There's no hidden, invisible soul. My brain, with its connections to my body, is me. My brain holds my memories, my hopes, and my dreams. And the same is true for you. So, it makes complete sense that taking good care of your body, and especially the brain that runs it, is of utmost importance.

If you're a Christian and think you should skip this short chapter because you believe in a soul and an afterlife, keep reading. What I have to say about taking care of yourself is important to you too—just not for the same exact reasons. Your Bible describes your body as a temple of the Holy Spirit. It teaches that all of you—including your body—belongs to God and that you've been entrusted to take care of what God has given you.[13]

So, even if you don't view this life as all there is like I do, it still makes sense to commit yourself to a healthy lifestyle. It makes sense to educate yourself on how you need to eat, how you need to sleep, and the kind of exercise you require. And it makes sense to put what you learn into practice.

Nobody's perfect. Do the best you can. Work with what you've got. Strive for some level of consistency. When you get off track, don't beat yourself up, just get back on course.

Become the world's best authority on what your body and your brain need for optimum functioning.

Treat your body like a priceless, irreplaceable automobile you've been given to keep your whole life—with the understanding that you can't get another one.

If you need to go to a doctor, pick the best one you can find and afford, and go. If financial problems make medical help seem out of reach, be relentless in your search for individuals or organizations that will help you find a way to get the care you need. Don't give up.

If something's broken and it can't be fixed, be as positive as you can about it. Find your own unique ways to keep moving forward in life despite physical limitations.

Life Principle

Health Matters: Take care of your body. You won't get another one, and you can't keep moving forward without it.

Serenity

The Serenity Prayer is used by participants in Alcoholics Anonymous and other 12-Step groups as an ever-present tool for keeping things in perspective. The prayer reads as follows:

> God grant me the serenity to accept the things I cannot change, the courage to change the things I can, and the wisdom to know the difference.[14]

I learned the value of The Serenity Prayer while working on recovery as an adult child of an alcoholic for five days in 1988 at The Meadows, a treatment center in Arizona. I was still a pastor at the time, and the experience was life-changing. The recovery process made me more aware of the need to acknowledge the things I could and could not control. And it reminded me to ask God for help with this task.

As a Christian, a foundational principle of my faith was the belief that God is in control. I believed that in the big scheme of things, nothing outside his permissive will could or would happen. So, The Serenity Prayer wasn't just a reminder of what I could or couldn't change. It was also a reminder that God was in control.

Even with my strong faith, having grown up in a home where alcoholism was present, I had a keen dislike of things feeling out of control, and that made The Serenity Prayer especially meaningful to me.

Now, I don't believe any God is in control of things or is available to grant me serenity. I have no promises to claim about what will or won't happen. It was a big leap from believing God has the whole world in his hands to the decision that no God exists.

When I left my faith, I had to acquiesce to a greater possibility that things might get out of control, and prayer was no longer an option.

As you've seen more than once in the preceding pages, I have no problem with secularizing and repurposing practical tools for meaningful living from religious sources—something that is especially easy to do with The Serenity Prayer. Creating my secular version was simple. I changed "God grant me" to "I seek."

> *I seek* the serenity to accept the things I cannot change, the courage to change the things I can, and the wisdom to know the difference

It's no longer a prayer, but in my view, it works just as well as when I used it as a prayer. A secular mindset increases the need for getting comfortable with a lack of control over what happens in life and, if anything, admitting what I cannot change is now even more empowering.

Navigating relationships, dealing with toxic thinking patterns, coping with suffering, evil, and danger in our world, and managing our health concerns all cry out for a serenity that comes from being wise about what we can change and what we can't. And the insight conveyed by a simple parable is relevant: A couple on vacation noticed an older fellow sitting on a porch in a rocking chair and emanating peacefulness, so much so that they asked him his secret. His reply: When it rains, I let it.

Regardless of your perspective on faith, I recommend the habit of remembering that some things are beyond our control. There's something peaceful about letting go of what you're only pretending to oversee. There's something empowering about seeking the courage to change what can be changed. And it's good to remind yourself that wisdom is often required to know what you can and cannot alter.

Meaningful living takes a hit whenever we exhaust ourselves by wrestling with situations that will never respond to our efforts. With wisdom, we can determine when letting go is the best way to take hold of the situation, and when our best efforts can change things for the better.

Life Principle

Serenity Matters: Seek the serenity to accept the things you cannot change, the courage to change the things you can, and the wisdom to know the difference.

Inspiration

Inspiration may be hard to define, but one thing is certain. Inspiration touches the core of what makes us able to find meaning. Inspiration breathes life into us and helps us to keep moving forward.

When I walked away from faith, I did not lose my hunger for inspiration. With the Bible, Christian music, and sermons no longer available to me as avenues of inspiration, I learned to be more open to finding it from other sources.

I recently watched news footage of Elon Musk's rocket pushing into space, launching his Tesla convertible into orbit—one more phase toward developing a spacecraft that will fly to Mars. It felt like another giant step for humanity, and I was inspired.

But accomplishments don't have to be headline-worthy to inspire. We can be inspired by anyone who refuses to give up and somehow manages to beat the odds.

One of my favorite TV shows is *America's Got Talent*. I don't think I've ever watched an episode without my eyes watering up. I'm inspired by people who put it all on the line in front of millions of viewers. It's often a singer who's survived a difficult journey to the stage, is there despite feeling vulnerable and afraid, and performs with incredible talent and passion that inspires me the most.

I love stories of people who do things family, friends, and peers never thought they could do. Such accounts inspire me to face my own challenges with strength and to live my own life with courage.

I can also be inspired by my interactions with nature, by great works of art, by music, and by the stories told through books and film.

I recently watched the movie, *The Post*, an account of the owner and editor of *The Washington Post* grappling with a decision of whether to publish classified material about the Vietnam War in 1971—information the public needed to know. It was an issue of freedom of the press. The owner and the editor of the paper risked prison if they published the information, but they did it anyway.

At one point in the movie, as the final decision to publish was being made, I couldn't keep the tears from welling up in my eyes. I was inspired by the courage and commitment of *The Washington Post* team to making sure American citizens knew the truth about the war.

What inspires you? What brings a tear to your eye and a lump to your throat? Make it a priority to include such things in your weekly routine.

Inspiration can recharge your sense of expectancy. Inspiration can reinforce your values. It can encourage you to rid yourself of toxic thinking. It can give you courage in the face of danger. Inspiration can motivate you to keep trudging along no matter how hard taking the next step has become.

Regardless of what inspires you, one of the most important results will be that you'll find it easier to keep moving toward meaning.

Life Principle

Inspiration Matters: Inspiration breathes life into us and helps us to keep moving toward meaning. Make it a priority to include things that inspire in your weekly routine.

Mantra

I've now shared my full list of life principles and core values that matter in a meaning-driven lifestyle. Join me in a quick review.

Seeking Truth Matters: Look deeper, be willing to change your mind, and follow the truth wherever it leads.

Self-Awareness Matters: Never stop learning about who you are—even when doing so is challenging or painful.

Values Matter: Build personal character on core values that work for everyone.

> **Strength**: Visualize your inner core of strength and practice strength training to build integrity, self-reliance, determination, and resilience.

> **Kindness**: Keep building your kindness quotient as you practice respect, empathy, patience, and forgiveness while remembering that kindness works best in partnership with confident inner strength.

Truthfulness: Tell the truth with strength, courage, and kindness.

Humility: Humility is the opposite of arrogance, and it's about keeping your perspective on who you are in the whole scheme of things.

Gratitude: Remember that you are not the source of everything that is valuable in your life and make a habit of being grateful for all the good that comes your way.

Generosity: Practice a generosity that flows from a positive, confident attitude. It's an admirable way to live. But remember that you get to decide how generous you want to be.

Love: Let love happen naturally. You don't have to love someone if you don't want to. Just remember to be kind to everyone as much as humanly possible. And when love happens, don't be frightened by it and run away.

Purpose Matters: Meaning comes from pursuing a value-driven purpose you are passionate about. Find and follow your own unique purpose in life.

Expectancy Matters: Choose to believe that something

good lies ahead. You're more likely not to miss something good when you're looking for it.

Pacing Matters: Pace yourself in life's journey—walking, being still, running, and flying—all have their place.

Now Matters: Cultivate a mindset of living in the present tense, checking periodically for recurring *conscious participation required* experiences like laughter, play, beauty, and wonderment.

Relationships Matter: Value each relationship for what it is and do the things that enable relationships to grow. Engage in active listening. Be honest, open, and vulnerable. Practice accountability. Connect with a community. Live boundary-sensitive.

Toxic Thinking Matters: Let go of all forms of toxic thinking. Check for the presence of toxic shame, guilt, fear, and hatred. Get help if you need it.

Danger Matters: Don't give in to fear but be realistic about life's dangers. Do what you can to protect yourself and others from harm.

Health Matters: Take care of your body. You won't get another one, and you can't keep moving forward without it.

Serenity Matters: Seek the serenity to accept the things you cannot change, the courage to change the things you can, and the wisdom to know the difference.

Inspiration Matters: Inspiration breathes life into us and helps us to keep moving toward meaning. Make it a priority to include things that inspire in your weekly routine.

Although this summary of principles and values that matter in a meaning-driven lifestyle is not that long, it's still a lot to remember. And what's important is not simply learning the list but putting what's in the list into practice.

This is a good time for a confession on my part: I do not implement these principles and values with 100% consistency. In fact, I'd rather not estimate my success rate in terms of a percentage. These are life *goals* for me—things I have to keep working on day by day.

With the challenge of successfully focusing on things that matter in mind, I decided a simple statement that sums up these principles and values in a couple of lines—a meaning mantra—would be helpful to me and to anyone else attempting to implement these concepts in day-to-day living. Here's how I constructed my self-talk meaning mantra.

Seeking the truth—wanting to understand things as they really are and working to know yourself—requires that you **dig deep**.

Yearning for what is highest and best in life requires that

you **aim high**.

And because NOW is when and where life happens, it makes sense to **find your best self in the present moment**.

A quick reminder is in order here: Finding your best self in the present moment doesn't mean you only think about now. Sometimes your best self in the present moment is a self that is reflecting on and learning from past experiences. Sometimes your best self in the present moment is a self that is considering what steps toward growth can be taken tomorrow or next month or next year. But most of the time, finding your best self in the present moment means being in the present moment.

Here's how the three statements fit together:

Dig deep. Aim high. Find your best self in the present moment.

There's one more thing. To find meaning in day-to-day living, we must **connect**. This means fully engaging with the richness of human relationships, the joys of life's beauty and wonder, and the helpful resources that are available to us. When you recognize the value and power of connecting, it makes sense to engage in frequent checkups:

- What connections in my life are broken, and what can I do to repair them?

- What new connections are waiting for me?
- What connections do I need to initiate or plan?
- Am I missing a positive connection that is begging to happen?

Now, let's add the connecting concept to complete the meaning mantra:

Dig deep. Aim high. Find your best self in the present moment. Connect.

I find it helpful to talk to myself using this mantra, or some part of it, in a way that applies one or more of the life principles and core values and to whatever challenge I might be facing.

If I'm having a difficult conversation with a person I love, I can say to myself, "Find your kind and caring self in the present moment. Don't let hurt or anger break this connection, even temporarily."

If I'm interacting with a sales or service person and notice that my mind is somewhere else, I can challenge myself, "Find the part of you that values relationships at every level. Initiate a friendly connection."

When life looks dreary and feels exhausting, I can tell myself, "Self-resuscitate. Find the you that loves laughter, beauty, and play. Do something that will pull you into the goodness of life in the present moment."

Mantra

If I'm feeling toxic shame, I can say to myself, "Dig deep. Find your shame-free self in the present moment. Connect with the emotional healing work you've done."

When I'm feeling afraid, I can say, "Dig deep. Aim high. Find your courageous self in the present moment. Connect with your inner core of strength."

If I'm having trouble getting on task, I may tell myself, "Find your purposeful self in the present moment. Connect with the why behind the task."

If I'm having trouble slowing down, I can tell myself, "Dig deep. Find your quiet, calm, and peaceful self in the present moment. Connect with your breathing."

At other times, I may just remind myself of the mantra or a part of it. I may tell myself, "Find your best self in the present moment," or "Connect," or "Aim high," or "Dig deep."

If you want to make the meaningful living principles and core values in this book a driving force in how you think and live, I recommend that you re-read this chapter frequently. And I recommend that you make the meaning mantra a frequently used reminder.

Dig deep. Aim high. Find your best self in the present moment.

Epilogue

After walking away from my prepackaged belief system, I faced a multitude of choices about what the new version of me would look like. I began to think for myself about how to build a meaningful life without God, faith, or religion, and this became a process of carefully considering what mattered to me in life.

I decided that if I could describe a religion-not-required way of finding meaning in life by focusing on things that really matter, it would be something worth sharing—especially if it could make sense and work for anyone, regardless of religious beliefs, political stance, personality type, lifestyle, or generational label. That's what I've attempted in this book.

I hope this read has already become a launching pad for your own consideration of what matters most, and I hope it has offered you some helpful ideas on how to live a more intentional and more meaningful life.

To find more helpful resources for meaningful living, visit me at MovingTruths.com.

Endnotes

[1] Robert Fulghum, *All I Really Need to Know, I Learned in Kindergarten: Uncommon Thoughts on Common Things* (New York: Ballantine Books, 2004), 10.

[2] "MBTI Basics," The Myers & Briggs Foundation Website, https://www.myersbriggs.org/my-mbti-personality-type/mbti-basics/home.htm?bhcp=1, Accessed August 11, 2019.

[3] M. Scott Peck, *People of the Lie: The Hope for Healing Human Evil* (New York: Simon and Schuster, 1983), 242.

[4] Mark 12:28-30.

[5] If this is the case with you, consider finding a qualified professional counselor who can help you with a plan for developing new relationships with people who are emotionally safe, people with whom you can be honest, open, and vulnerable. Don't let the lack of funds deter you. Be proactive. Some counselors will occasionally work with a client for a dramatically reduced rate as an act of service. Community counseling services may be available. If you cannot find a counselor, look for free support groups that can offer help.

[6] Adam Lee, "Why People Are Flocking to a New Wave of Secular Communities: Atheist Churches, https://www.alternet.org/belief/why-people-are-flocking-new-wave-secular-communities-atheist-churches, November 27, 2013. "About Oasis," Oasis Network Website,

https://www.peoplearemoreimportant.org/about-oasis.
Sunday Assembly Website, https://www.sundayassembly.com/story.
New Unity Website, https://www.new-unity.org.

[7] "Latest Crime Statistics Released: Increase in Violent Crime, Decrease in Property Crime," FBI Website, September 26, 2016. https://www.fbi.gov/news/stories/latest-crime-statistics-released.

[8] Martha Stout, *The Sociopath Next Door: The Ruthless Versus the Rest of Us* (New York: Broadway Books, 2005).

[9] Marie E. Rueve and Randon S. Welston, "Violence and Mental Illness," Psychiatry MMC, May 2008, online article: https://www.ncbi.nlm.nih.gov/pmc/articles/PMC2686644.

[10] "Alcohol Use Disorder (AUD) in the United States" and "Alcohol Related Deaths," National Institute on Alcohol Abuse and Alcoholism, https://www.niaaa.nih.gov/alcohol-health/overview-alcohol-consumption/alcohol-facts-and-statistics, citing A.H. Mokdad, J.S. Marks, D.F. Stroup, and J.L. Gerberding, "Actual causes of death in the United States 2000," [Published erratum in: *JAMA* 293(3):293–294, 298] *JAMA: Journal of the American Medical Association* 291(10):1238–1245, 2004. PMID: 15010446.

[11] "Child Abuse Statistics & Facts," *Childhelp*, citing C.W. Harlow, "Prior Abuse Reported by Inmates and Probationers," Washington, DC: US Dept. of Justice, Office of Justice Programs, Bureau of Justice Statistics, 1999. https://www.childhelp.org/child-abuse-statistics/?gclid=EAIaIQobChMIiJL4w-3Q2AIVBbnACh1yrwxiEAAYAyAAEgIkQPD_BwE.

[12] M. Scott Peck, *People of the Lie: The Hope for Healing Human Evil* (New York: Simon and Schuster, 1983), 223-226.

[13] 1 Corinthians 6:19.

[14] Reinhold Neibuhr (1892-1971).

www.ingramcontent.com/pod-product-compliance
Lightning Source LLC
Chambersburg PA
CBHW031355040426
42444CB00005B/300